SUBMARINES IN COMBAT

THE WATTS SEAPOWER LIBRARY

SUBMARINES IN COMBAT

Compiled by

Joseph B. Icenhower,

Rear Admiral U.S.N., Ret.

FRANKLIN WATTS, INC.
575 Lexington Avenue, New York 22

ACKNOWLEDGMENTS

The selections in this book are used by permission and specal arrangements with the proprietors of their respective copyrights who are listed below. The editor's and publisher's thanks to all who made this collection possible.

The editor and publisher have made every effort to trace the ownership of all material contained herein. It is their belief that the necessary permissions from publishers, authors, and authorized agents have been obtained in all cases. In the event of any questions arising as to the use of any material, the editor and publisher express regret for any error unconsciously made and will be pleased to make the necessary correction in future editions of this book.

Army Times Publishing Company for excerpts from THEY FOUGHT UNDER THE SEA, by the Editors of Navy Times, © 1962 by the Army Times Publishing Co.

Ballantine Books, Inc. for excerpts from U-BOATS AT WAR, by Harald Busch, © 1955 by Harald Busch.

D. C. Benson & Campbell Thomson, Ltd. for excerpts from STANDBY TO SURFACE, by Richard Baxter, published by Cassell & Co., Ltd.

William Morrow & Co., Inc. for excerpts from CHALLENGERS OF THE DEEP, by Wilbur Cross, published by William Sloane Associates, © 1959 by William Morrow & Co., Inc.

Harry Regnery Co., Publishers, for excerpts from TWENTY MILLION TONS UNDER THE SEA, by Rear Admiral Dan Gallery, U.S.N., © 1956 by Henry Regnery Co., and for excerpts from SEA DEVILS, by J. Valerio Borghese, © 1954 by Henry Regnery Co.

United States Naval Institute, for excerpts from the following:

U.S. SUBMARINE OPERATIONS IN WORLD WAR II, copyright © 1949 by U. S. Naval Institute, Annapolis, Maryland.

"I Sank the *Yorktown* at Midway," by Yahachi Tanabe with Joseph D. Harrington, from the May 1963 *Proceedings*, copyright © 1963 by U. S. Naval Institute.

"Stalking the *Takao* in Singapore Harbor," by Charles G. Kittredge, from the April 1957 *Proceedings*, copyright © 1957 by U. S. Naval Institute.

"404 Days. The War Patrol Life of German U505," by Hans J. Decker, from the March 1960 *Proceedings*, copyright © 1960 by U. S. Naval Institute.

A. P. Watt & Son for excerpts from BY GUESS AND BY GOD, by William Guy Carr, © 1930 by The Hutchinson Publishing Group.

The World Publishing Co. for excerpts from NAUTILUS 90 NORTH, by Commander William R. Anderson and Clay Blair, Jr., © 1959 by World Publishing Co.

Contents

SUBMARINES IN COMBAT

Introduction

SUBMARINE warfare is enthusiastically endorsed by many, loudly damned by many, and abhorred by all. It is an ungallant means of war, but there is no gallant warfare in modern times. Moreover, submarine warfare is effective. It is effective because of the type of men who go under the sea to fight.

Submarines in Combat is a book about these men. More specifically, it is a book about commanding officers, their courage and their fears, but above all, their often frightening responsibility.

Comdr. Lawson P. Ramage, carrot-topped terror of the Japanese, received the Congressional Medal of Honor for the second patrol of the USS Parche in July of 1944. The following excerpt from the monograph recommending Commander Ramage for the Congressional Medal of Honor will show what is necessary to be a recipient of this coveted award:

THE PERSONAL DARING AND OUTSTANDING SKILL DISPLAYED BY THE COMMANDING OFFICER IN HIS SERIES OF ATTACKS AGAINST A LARGE, HEAVILY ESCORTED ENEMY CONVOY, CONSISTING OF TANKERS, TRANSPORTS, AND FREIGHTERS, CONTACTED ON 31 JULY, IS ONE OF THE OUTSTANDING ATTACKS IN THE SUBMARINE WARFARE TO DATE, WITH ACTION PACKED INTO EVERY MINUTE OF THIS FORTY-SIX MINUTE BATTLE AGAINST THE ENEMY. ATTAINING THE ULTIMATE IN AGGRESSIVENESS, EXCEPTIONAL COURAGE, PERSONAL HEROISM, AND BEARING, THE COMMANDING OFFICER SAGACIOUSLY AND WITH CONSUMMATE SKILL, FIRED NINETEEN TORPEDOES IN FORTY-SIX MINUTES TO OBTAIN FOURTEEN OR FIFTEEN HITS IN THIS BRILLIANT NIGHT SURFACE ATTACK.

BY A BRILLIANT ACT OF STRATAGEM THE COMMANDING OFFICER PENETRATED THE STRONG ESCORT SCREEN; AND, ALTHOUGH HEMMED IN ON ALL SIDES BY SHIPS AND ESCORTS TRYING TO MANEUVER AND DELIVER COUNTERATTACKS, HE DARINGLY CLOSED TO A FAVORABLE FIRING POSITION FROM WHICH TO LAUNCH HIS TORPEDOES. WITH A WELL EXECUTED STERN SHOT, HE SUCCEEDED IN DAMAGING A FREIGHTER. FOLLOWING UP WITH A SERIES OF BOW AND STERN SHOTS, HE SANK THE LEADING TANKER AND DAMAGED A SECOND TANKER. DESPITE THE GRAVE PROBLEM OF MACHINE-GUN FIRE AND FLARES FROM ESCORTS, NEAR PROXIMITY OF VESSELS, SOME AS CLOSE AS 200 YARDS, HE SUCCESSFULLY DELIVERED TWO FORWARD RELOADS TO SINK A TRANSPORT. AT THE SAME TIME, HE COMMENCED MANEUVERING TO AVOID NEAREST ESCORT'S GUNFIRE AND OBTAIN A STERN SHOT AT DAMAGED TANKER THAT HAD NOW MANNED HER GUNS. AS HE REACHED A FIRING POSITION, THE FIRST FUSILLADE OF TANKER'S 4" OR 5" SHELLS PASSED CLOSE OVERHEAD AND SLIGHTLY FORWARD. BECAUSE OF THE ACCURACY AND INTENSE FIREPOWER OF ADDITIONAL ENEMY 20 MM. AND 40 MM. INCREASING THE POSSIBILITIES OF CASUALTIES, ALL LOOKOUTS AND SPARE HANDS WERE SENT BELOW, WITH THE EXCEPTION OF THE BRIDGE QUARTERMASTER WHO VOLUNTEERED TO REMAIN ON THE TBT. THE COMMANDING OFFICER, WITH UTTER DISREGARD FOR PERSONAL SAFETY, COURAGEOUSLY REMAINED AT HIS STATION, ON THE BRIDGE, DESPITE THE HAIL OF BULLETS AND SHELLS, IN ORDER TO MANEUVER HIS SHIP MORE EFFECTIVELY AND SCORE HITS WITH HIS STERN TUBES. SIMULTANEOUSLY WITH HIS SINKING THE DAMAGED TANKER AND WHILE TRYING TO CLOSE A LARGE TRANSPORT, HE WAS FORCED TO COMMENCE EVASIVE MANEUVERS TO AVOID A FAST

3

TRANSPORT OR FREIGHTER BEARING DOWN, APPARENTLY INTENT ON RAM-
MING HIM, AND ALSO IN ORDER TO AVOID CONCENTRATED MACHINE-GUN
FIRE OF THE TWO NEARBY ESCORTS. WITH BULLETS AND SHELLS FLYING
ALL AROUND, HE ORDERED EMERGENCY FULL SPEED AHEAD AND SWUNG
THE STERN OF *PARCHE* AS SHE CROSSED THE BOW OF THE ONRUSHING
TRANSPORT OR FREIGHTER, CLEARING THIS ENEMY SHIP BY LESS THAN FIFTY
FEET!

ALTHOUGH NOW BOXED IN BY ESCORTS AND THE LARGE TRANSPORT
DEAD AHEAD, THE COMMANDING OFFICER DELIVERED THREE SMASHING
DOWN-THE-THROAT BOW SHOTS AND STOPPED THE TARGET. WITH HIGH
SPEED AND EXPERT SEAMANSHIP, HE TENACIOUSLY ATTACKED AGAIN, SCORING
A KILLING HIT WITH A RELOADED STERN TORPEDO.

AT BREAK OF DAWN, WITH ENEMY ESCORTS' COUNTER-ATTACKS BECOMING
TOO ACCURATE TO JUSTIFY FURTHER ATTACK AND RISK, *PARCHE* CLEARED
THE AREA, THUS HAVING DAMAGED ONE ENEMY SHIP AND SUNK FOUR
OTHERS IN FORTY-SIX MINUTES. IN ANOTHER ENCOUNTER, A 300 TON PATROL
VESSEL WAS SUNK BY GUNFIRE.

THE COUNTER-ATTACKS OF THE ENEMY AGAINST *PARCHE* DURING HER
SERIES OF AGGRESSIVE SURFACE TORPEDO ATTACKS UPON THE CONVOY ON
31 JULY 1944 WERE PROBABLY THE MOST INTENSIVE AND THOROUGH COUN-
TER-ATTACKS EVER ENCOUNTERED BY A SUBMARINE ENGAGED IN SURFACE
APPROACHES AND ATTACKS AGAINST THE ENEMY. ONLY EXCEPTIONAL SEA-
MANSHIP, OUTSTANDING PERSONAL HEROISM AND EXTREME BRAVERY OF
PARCHE'S COMMANDING OFFICER SAVED THIS SUBMARINE FROM SERIOUS
DAMAGE IF NOT TOTAL DESTRUCTION BY ENEMY GUNFIRE AND RAMMING.

THE COMMANDING OFFICER'S COURAGE AND FEARLESS ACTIONS IN RE-
MAINING ON THE BRIDGE OF HIS SUBMARINE DURING INTENSE AND ACCU-
RATE ENEMY GUNFIRE IN ORDER TO MAINTAIN THE OFFENSIVE AT ALL
TIMES, ENABLED HIM TO CONTROL HIS SHIP SKILLFULLY AND EFFICIENTLY,
LAUNCH HIS TORPEDOES EFFECTIVELY AND EVADE THE ENEMY'S VIGOROUS
EFFORTS TO DESTROY *PARCHE*.

Ramage's Rampage

WILBUR CROSS

EVERY officer and man aboard the USS *Parche* was frustrated and disgusted, but perhaps no one more so than the submarine's skipper, Comdr. L. P. Ramage. From conning tower to engine room the word went the rounds, "The Old Man's in a hell of a mood." He was up there on the tiny bridge now, glowering into the night, his thoughts fiery enough to match the red hair that gave him the nickname "Captain Red."

The reason behind the frustration was that *Parche*, on her second war patrol in July, 1944, should have been boring in for a kill on some juicy Jap shipping. Instead, she was looping back and forth off Cape Engaño north of the Philippines chasing phantoms in what the crew caustically referred to as a "snipe hunt." A large Japanese convoy had been reported by sister ships of the *Parche*, but so far the sonarmen, radarmen, and lookouts had not picked up even the suspicion of a trail.

"It looks like a dull evening," muttered the port lookout as night began to fall on the thirtieth and the sea stretched on all sides placidly and seemingly unmolested by any other ships of war. "With a nice moon coming up, how'd you like to be out here paddling your girl in a canoe?"

By way of answer the starboard lookout spat over the side. It sure was frustrating to get a contact report secondhand and then not be able to raise so much as a blip on the radar screen. But there was no use talking about it. The Old Man looked unhappy enough as it was as he eased his tight, wiry frame down through the hatch manhole to see if radar had picked up anything yet.

The weeks, days, and hours of monotony were almost over. But no one aboard the *Parche* could have guessed how much so at the moment when the quartermaster wearily wrote "July 31, 0100, no

5

contact" in the logbook and wondered if they ever would get rid of their twenty-four fish during the patrol.

The USS *Parche*, along with the *Hammerhead* and *Steelhead*, made up a wolf pack known as "Parks' Pirates." The standard joke was that they should have been called the "Headhunters," since they were composed of *Hammerhead*, *Steelhead*, and (referring to Ramage) redhead. On this patrol they had been assigned to an area known as "Convoy College" lying between Luzon and Formosa and so called because it was the sector in which wolf packs like the Pirates and Mickey Finns received basic training in how to pick off Japanese ships. Formosa was the point of convergence of six main Jap convoy lanes—from the Nipponese mainland and Shanghai to the north, from Hong Kong and Hainan to the west, and from Singapore and the Palau Islands to the south. Any submarine assigned to these waters was bound to sight potential prizes belonging to the Japanese Co-Prosperity Sphere—all, that is, except the *Parche* on her second patrol, which seemed to be flunking badly. Although she had set out more than five weeks before, she had not yet expended a single torpedo.

At 10:30 in the morning, July 30, *Steelhead* had sighted distant smoke from a convoy but could get no closer to investigate because of the heavy umbrella of air protection. The Japanese were throwing everything they could in the path of the American forces advancing through the Marianas, and air cover always consisted of plenty of Jap pilots ready to use suicide tactics. After a frustrating day of his own, her skipper, Comdr. D. L. Whelchel, got off a message to Ramage, reporting the contact, figuring the *Parche* would be in a more advantageous position north of the convoy, where she could wait for darkness and slip in for an attack.

All that day and into the night the *Parche*'s radar and sonar probed the waters of the Philippine Sea with only one result: Captain Red grew more and more impatient. At midnight he stood on the bridge, squinting through his binoculars across water made milky white in some patches by the light of a waning moon. There was not a silhouette of any kind to be seen anywhere. Frustration was setting in fast.

"A position report from *Steelhead*, sir," came the radio operator's report at thirty minutes past midnight.

"Where?"

6

"The reported Japanese convoy has changed course and is now some 30 miles to the southeast of us."

"Come to course 140 degrees true," muttered Ramage. "If we don't make contact soon, half the crew will be putting in for transfer." The sky, which had been dotted with clouds, was becoming overcast, hiding the moon half of the time. The sky along the horizon looked squally.

At 0230 there was still no sign of the Japs, but at 0240 Ramage, discouraged because the moon was just setting and reducing his visibility to a few hundred yards, suddenly received a report that sent him hustling from the bridge down into the conning tower.

"Radar contact!"

"I've got to see it to believe it," said Ramage. He had full confidence in his chief electronics technician, John C. Gray, Jr., whom he referred to as "a fabulous guy and a master of precision," but he had been chasing ghosts so long he was ready to blow his redheaded top any minute. If he alerted the crew on another false alarm it would be sheer murder.

By the time he took one glance at the radar screen in the conning tower he was convinced, and at 0246 the general-quarters alarm sounded. The *Parche* began closing fast, guided by radar until a visual contact could be made. This came half an hour later when, through scattered rainsqualls, the dim shadows of Jap ships were picked up ahead. It was 0307.

By now the Japanese were fully alerted through their own radar and sonar devices. One of the escort ships fired warning flares signaling the convoy to begin evasive maneuvers and to aid the other escorts in converging on the enemy.

At this point commenced one of the most audacious engagements in the history of United States naval warfare as the lone 1,600-ton boat challenged and took on the entire convoy, any one of whose escorts, loaded with heavy armament, depth charges, and torpedoes, could have meant death to a submarine.

Even more remarkable than the nature of the lopsided fight was the unique manner in which Captain Red Ramage chose to attack.

Ramage had graduated from the Naval Academy in 1931 and been assigned directly to destroyers. He quickly became familiar with hit-and-run tactics and methods of taking advantage of superior speeds and maneuverability in pressing an attack. And he had

7

the temperament to go along with it. Ramage was not a big man, but he had the kind of fighting instinct that did justice to his red hair. When he made decisions, he made them fast, and accurately. He learned that a small ship that could catch a larger one off-balance and press the attack had a distinct advantage that out-weighed size alone. When he joined the submarine force, he never forgot what he had learned aboard the old cans.

At the time of contact, the *Parche* was proceeding south, with the convoy almost directly east of her. As Jap escorts closed in on the position where they knew the unseen submarine to be, Ramage tried a reverse spinner, heading west, then north, and finally east.

"By God, Captain, look where we are," said the executive officer, Lt. Comdr. Woodrow W. McCrory, when the maneuver had been completed. "The rascals have changed course and are headed right into our laps." There was a touch of gleefulness in his voice.

The submarine, charging at 20 knots, and still on the surface, was now well *inside* the ring of escort vessels with the bows of several freighters and tankers dead ahead, all coming due west while the *Parche* headed east.

"Clear the bridge!" shouted Ramage. The two lookouts and the duty officers vanished quickly below, leaving only the captain and his quartermaster, whose duty it was to assist with the visual navigation.

"Things are getting pretty hot up there," said one of the lookouts. "The Old Man must be ready to take her down."

The lean and fiery Ramage had no such intention. Nothing was going to make him submerge—not while Ensign Gray at the radar had picked up what he interpreted as an escort vessel at 6,000 yards, a second one at 12,000, and ten potential targets within a distance of 18,000 yards.

At 0354 *Parche* began closing on a medium AK cargo vessel, with the quartermaster, George G. Plume, Jr., taking rapid bearings through the TBT (target bearing transmitter, a sighting device which transmits the relative bearings of ships to the conning tower each time the operator presses his "mark" button). But she had appeared so quickly out of the darkness there was not time to complete the bearing and fire bow tubes.

"Hard right!" ordered Ramage from the open bridge. If the *Parche* kept on course she would have plowed right into the enemy.

8

As it was, she slid past with less than 200 yards to spare. Ramage's idea was to make a complete circle and head for her from behind, bringing his bow tubes to bear.

The Jap ship opened up with everything she had, and the sky was lit by streams of tracers and the flash of five-inchers.

"Let me know when you've got a firing setup," shouted Ramage into the intercom to the TDC (torpedo data computer) operator, Lt. F. W. Allcorn, Jr., his torpedo officer. "It's all lit up like Times Square up here."

"We've got it," replied Allcorn. "Target is tracking on the nose."

"Give her two," ordered Ramage. "That ought to put her out of misery."

Two torpedoes sped from the bow tubes, and the AK began a desperate turn, which suceeded in avoiding them. In doing so, however, she moved directly into the path of an escort vessel charging toward *Parche* and unintentionally blocked the escort's attack so that Ramage was free to select another target.

Torpedo Officer Allcorn, who had continued to track the AK until ordered otherwise, now found that the *Parche*'s 360-degree swing gave him another setup, this time on the after tubes.

"Give her one more for good measure, then," said Ramage. The third torpedo sped out into the black waters, this time finding the mark the other two had missed. In due time there was a dull explosion astern.

"I think we got her," said Ramage to Quartermaster Plume, but there was no time to stop for sight-seeing. Off to starboard, in the TBT sights, was what looked to be two small carriers in procession, but which immediately turned out to be tankers—juicy targets for any submariner. A scant three minutes later the *Parche* was closing in, bow pointed north.

"We've got the setup," said the torpedo officer, who had now switched targets, using the bearings from the quartermaster, and was "playing the organ" furiously—feeding range and bearing information into the torpedo data computer, which came up with the correct settings instantly.

"Hold her." Captain Red kept his eye on the silhouette of the closer of the two tankers as the *Parche*'s bow knifed into the seas at full speed, and her tail sent up a sheet of white spray. The submarine was spotted now. He could hear the sound of alarm bells and knew Jap gunners were trying to get a bead on their enemy.

"Two thousand yards . . . 1,500 . . . 1,100 . . ." The radar operator called off the range readings rapidly, as the distance closed fast.

"Fire one!" shouted Ramage as the computer delivered data on the enemy's port bow. Using slight starboard rudder, Ramage was letting his boat swing to the right, toward his second target. "Fire two!" That was aimed at the belly of tanker number one. "Fire three!" That should hit just about at the quarter. "Fire four!" And one for the stern. Tankers were tough targets at all times and this one was too juicy to take chances on a miss for any reason—miscalculations, misfires, changes in speed.

On tanker number one the *Parche* had a perfect score. The bow was blown off by the seventh torpedo of the evening. The midsection exploded with a blinding sheet of fire from torpedo number five. And numbers six and seven tore the stern sections in half. She plunged under the Pacific with hardly any slackening in speed, leaving nothing but a burning patch of oil to serve as a fine torch for silhouetting the following ship.

"Hard right," ordered Ramage, his bare red head wet from light spray and heavy sweat. The second tanker, which had not altered course, was now in range but so close there was no time to reload any of the six bow tubes. *Parche* swung neatly around until her stern was aimed at the target.

"We've got a setup in the after tubes," said the torpedo officer.

"Fire all of them," came the order. Ramage had already expended one of the four stern torpedoes, and the other three sped toward target. A minute later Ramage, hanging onto the grab rails on the weather bridge, cursed when he realized the first shot had missed. The next two struck the tanker forward, slowing her down but not stopping her completely. Not bad: of the ten torpedoes loaded in the ten tubes at the start of the battle, he had missed with only three.

By now every man on the boat, whether actively working or on emergency standby, was following the action audibly as orders flashed over the intercom in each section of the *Parche*.

"Well, I guess the Old Man will have to take her down now," said a rookie engineman, making his first patrol on the *Parche*.

10

"You want to bet?" asked a heavily bearded chief, without looking up from a bank of meters in the maneuvering room.

"Sure. That last salvo was numbers eight, nine, and ten. Six fish from the bow and four from the stern. What have you got left?"

The rookie engineman would have been right—except for one unique fact: Comdr. L. P. Ramage was about to make history. Months before, on his first patrol with the *Parche,* he had started training his torpedo-room crews in reloading torpedo tubes under the most extreme conditions, while the boat was making full speed on the surface, rolling and pitching, with the imminent possibility of having to crash-dive. Never before had this type of operation been tackled by submariners, the standard practice being to dive deep, level off, and run slowly when torpedoes were moved from stowage racks to loading cradles and thence into the tubes fore and aft.

The surface reload was not only extremely difficult but hazardous as well, for if a torpedo should get loose from its rack it would be a ton of unmanageable steel and explosives, crushing men and equipment like so many eggshells. On the *Parche*'s first patrol, Ramage had successfully loaded four torpedoes in the forward tubes while maneuvering on the surface for an attack.

Now, under more intensified battle conditions, and with the boat changing course frequently and at full speed, he was attempting the same surface reload maneuver. Once it got under way he would not be able to take the *Parche* down without considerable delay to make certain no torpedoes were loose enough to be rendered dangerous by the angle of dive.

Thus far in the engagement, Ramage had brazenly ignored the escort vessels which were probably echoing with Japanese profanity. The *Parche*'s unexpected speed and maneuverability on the surface and the extreme daring of her skipper kept the Japs outguessed at every turn. Whenever an escort would get a bearing on the *Parche*— an unusually difficult feat since she was one of the first boats to be painted a camouflage gray instead of the normally accepted black— one of the ungainly old *marus* milling around would bumble into her path. But even so, Ramage's position was being scorched by heavy automatic weapons fire, enough so that he kept getting madder and madder at the Japs all around him and refused to leave the bridge under any circumstances.

11

Down in the control room, the man at the Christmas tree, the board on which red and green lights indicated which valves were open and which shut, sat with sweat pouring down his face. "Upstairs," through the hatch, he could hear the thunder of enemy guns and often the tattoo of smaller-caliber bullets along the steel superstructure. The diving officer, Lt. David H. Green, was rigged for diving the instant the order came down to the conning tower, but somehow he knew it would not come. Captain Red was having too much of a field day to give up now, with fourteen torpedoes left aboard.

"What's the matter with the Old Man?" a seaman asked nervously. "Are you sure he's still alive up there?"

Lieutenant Commander McCrory laughed, as hot steel rained overhead. He knew damned well Ramage had no intention of taking her down. As executive officer, he had been given a loose assignment as a free agent, wandering from compartment to compartment to check any snags in operations. No five men in other parts of the boat seemed as busy as any one man in the two torpedo rooms. Theirs was a labor of pure love as they heaved and sweated the torpedoes, as slippery as greased pigs, into the tubes. The hull rang with the clank of chain falls and bars and the muffled slamming of tube doors, as the deadly fish were slid into position.

"Well, lads," said the exec, "this is what we've been looking for. We're going for broke this time."

On the bridge Ramage had a few rough moments after the original ten fish had gone. How were the boys making out down below? He did not have long to think about it, because Quartermaster Plume was calmly lining up a medium-sized *maru* in the TBT. Ramage steadied himself with both hands outstretched on the grab rails, freckled face low and close to the intercom so that he could bark orders into it.

"More speed!" he shouted to the engine-room gang. "Give me everything you've got." He had to get to the *maru* before an escort got to the *Parche*.

"We can't squeeze another quarter knot out of her, sir," came the reply. "We're on flank already." What did the Old Man think he was doing—still riding one of those crazy cans?

"OK, OK. Forward torpedo room, how's the reload?"

"We've got two in, Captain."

12

"Stand by, then." The *maru* loomed closer. The torpedo officer had the setup now on the TDC. "Fire two!"

"Two torps on their way," came the reply an instant later. "We're commencing full reload."

"Left full rudder!" shouted Ramage, as the *Parche* started getting uncomfortably blistered by deck gunfire from the *maru*. The *Parche*'s new gray camouflage job was serving its purpose well, but the Jap gunners could still sight on the white fin of spray rising from the submarine's tail as she continued at top speed. "And make ready all tubes."

The *Parche* slewed around to port and away from target. A few seconds later came the two dull explosions that gave the submarine a satisfying shudder and aroused battle cheers from everyone aboard. The Japanese merchantman had taken both fish squarely in her guts. Jerry-built for war service, she simply broke in two. The tracers from her batteries fore and aft skewed crazily, those in the bow rising skyward and those in the stern *ping*ing into the sea as the two halves of the ship tilted inward and began to sink.

"We're ready to take her down any time you are," came a report from the control room to the bridge when Ramage announced they could chalk up another kill. Escorts were boring in now from several approaches.

"Hang on a bit longer," said Commander Ramage, his lean jaw thrust out with determination. He still had twelve torpedoes aboard. Thus far at least that destroyer training back in the early thirties had really paid off. It was doubtful any of the brass supervising those training courses in night torpedo attacks against cruisers and battleships would have dreamed the tactics could be used by anything but destroyers.

While the officers and men below sweated and labored at assignments no submariners in history had ever been called upon to perform, Ramage calmly completed his reverse spinner so he could head back again for tanker number two, which was still afloat despite the two fish that had struck her forward. Down in the conning tower, where some fourteen officers and men concentrated on their jobs, Seaman First Class Courtland C. Stanton was getting a little dizzy. Stationed at the wheel, he had spun it for so many "hard rights" and "hard lefts," so many spinners, and so many changes of compass direction, he felt like a cross-eyed man on a merry-go-round.

13

Ramage had to make a quick decision now—which suited his flaming temperament just right. *Parche* was headed due north at full speed, the tanker due west and about 2,000 yards off his port bow. He could not wait for the reload in the bow tubes, but the after torpedo room reported it had three fish reloaded. Captain Red decided bold tactics were the best—he would bore right in under the tanker's stern, which was high in the water because of the sinking bow, then loose his stern tubes from the other side.

In a confusing montage of flaring oil and flashing tracers, the *Parche* passed directly under her stern while the surprised Jap gunners feverishly tried to break loose their after mount, jammed from the angle of the deck. Some 500 yards beyond target, as *Parche* "opened out" for a stern shot, the stricken tanker fired every gun she had. It looked for a few seconds as though Ramage had pushed his luck too far. But he had estimated his chances with the cool precision of an officer who has had a dozen years of tactical experience. His surprise maneuver was just radical enough, and the tanker's inclination just critical enough, so that none of her hot metal struck home in time.

"You got the setup?" asked the skipper impatiently after he had maneuvered *Parche*'s tail to bear on the tanker, like a scorpion preparing for a sting.

"Yes, sir," replied Torpedo Officer Allcorn.

"After torp room, look lively!"

"We're ready with three, sir," came the reply.

"Half speed," ordered Ramage. The engine-room telegraph clanged and there was a noticeable slackening in the boat's forward sprint. Firing torpedoes at anything above 10 knots was a tricky business because of the speed factor in computing. Yet Ramage had challenged all precedent by firing his forward torpedoes at full speed—forcing them into the wall of water formed by the bow's 20-knot lunge ahead. When it came to firing stern torpedoes, he had to slow to about 10 knots so they would not have too much backward momentum at the instant of leaving the tubes.

"Half speed," repeated the engine room.

"OK, after torp room, don't wait for invitations." Three fish raced from the *Parche*'s stern tubes, boiling along unseen about 25 feet below the surface of the dark Pacific. The range was 800 yards.

"One cigar! Two cigars! Three cigars!" The men howled with delight as each dull impact was transmitted through the water. The tanker, already crippled by the two haymakers in her bow, slid without protest under the waves, leaving behind nothing but burning fuel.

Ramage was beginning to feel a sense of accomplishment now, as he mentally computed all pertinent facts: he had just expended torpedoes thirteen, fourteen, and fifteen. How many would the forward torpedo room have in the process of reload now?

Suddenly, as he concentrated on these things, a black shadow loomed off the starboard bow, a small, fast *maru* bearing down on the *Parche* with intent to ram.

"Enginehouse!" shouted Ramage. "Pour on all the oil you've got. I feel like a mouse at a bridge party up here!"

The *Parche* had now regained full speed, but Ramage saw he needed flank speed and then some to pull off his next maneuver. As he plunged directly northward, the *maru* bore in from the east, spraying automatic weapons fire.

The gap closed fast . . . 300 yards, 200 yards. Now she was scarcely as far away as the *Parche's* own length, headed for the submarine's conning tower and bridge from directly abeam. Ramage glowered calmly at this instrument of destruction, like a bullfighter standing in defiance of a charging animal.

"Hard right! Emergency!"

Seaman First Class Stanton at the wheel was by this time thoroughly familiar in the techniques of operating the *Parche* like a PT boat. The *maru* passed by on Ramage's starboard side as the forward half of the submarine cleared her bows and the latter half slewed around with the agility of a water skier making a right-angle turn.

The Japanese officers and deck men were screaming first with jubilation when it looked like a sure bet that they would cut the submarine in two, then with frustration as *Parche* slid by. So close was the maneuver that there was less than 50 feet to spare.

The *Parche* was now boxed in on all sides by Japanese small craft and escorts, all firing indiscriminately and so close they must undoubtedly have done a good bit of overshooting and damaged their own ships. But Ramage's maneuver had been coldly calculated, and Quartermaster Plume, swallowing hard, could see why the skipper had taken the gamble of holding course until he got past the would-be rammer. Dead ahead lay a large AP troop transport vessel.

15

"By God, sir, she's a honey," said the quartermaster. Since the Japanese vessel was coming bow-on and the *Parche* was such a narrow target, the Jap gunners could not depress their guns enough to let loose any heavy stuff. It was a tricky position for attack. Torpedoes would have to be aimed with extreme accuracy to make a strike.

"Bow torpedo room," Ramage spoke calmly into the intercom, "how many fish do you have ready?"

"Three, sir," came the reply, the talker gasping a little for breath this time. It must have been 125 degrees in the torpedo rooms, with the deck slippery from dripping sweat. "But . . . we'll have a fourth secured . . . in a minute." The men were stripped to their skivvies.

"No time," said Ramage. "Stand by for three."

Ramage waited a few seconds as range and bearing estimates were flashed from the radar operator and the quartermaster at the TBT. So much at close quarters was the action during the entire engagement that at one point John Gray, the chief electronics technician, one of the coolest, most methodical men Ramage had ever seen under high pressure, had actually shut off the set to retune it because he complained that it was "25 yards off."

"OK, Captain, I've got the setup," said Torpedo Officer Allcorn on the torpedo data computer.

"Fire one!" shouted Ramage. Both vessels continued to hold course, the troop transport probably because she offered a smaller target than if she should turn broadside and because she, too, was intent on ramming.

"Check your setup again," said Ramage, slapping the coaming with the broad palm of his hand. "That baby missed."

"Fire two! Fire three!" rang out as the *Parche* continued to close the range. The torpedoes sped straight down the transport's throat. "Left full rudder, before we get run over!" The submarine, swinging away from the starboard bow, shuddered as the two fish struck home.

Captain Red still was not satisfied. That miss—only the fourth out of eighteen shots—had made him mad, and the big transport, though well down at the bow, looked as though she might still float long enough for the Japanese troops aboard to reach safety. The bow tubes were now empty, but the after torpedo room had one in its tube and ready to go.

Ramage slowed speed slightly as the *Parche* arced some 800 yards away from the big transport, then gave the firing order.

The seconds went by. Ramage gripped the coaming edge and counted to himself. Quartermaster Plume lifted his eyes from his sights to look back past the white fin of spray marking the *Parche's* tail. Then came a thundering *wharroom!* and a flash directly amidships. There followed a weird clanging of deck machinery and the hollow reverberations of loose chunks of metal and equipment crashing about inside the enemy transport. Then she plunged beneath the waves. The time was 0442.

The only ships within range now were heavily armed escort vessels, all concentrating their fury on the *Parche* since there seemed to be nothing left of their own convoy to endanger by indiscriminate fire. It was getting too hot even for Captain Red and besides, with nineteen torpedoes gone, he only had five left in case he spotted a more worthy target during the remainder of his patrol. Reluctantly he decided to haul clear.

"Set course 330 degrees true, and let's put a little distance between us and this hornet's nest," he called down to the conning tower. "Dawn's beginning to break."

"Take her down," said the diving officer, wiping the sweat from his brow with relief at the order everyone had expected long before this.

As the dark Pacific changed to a mass of foam across the forward decks, Quartermaster Plume squeezed lithely through the manhole, followed immediately by Ramage. Behind them the hatch slammed shut, cutting out the din of gunfire beyond. Ramage spun the wheel tight and stepped from the ladder to the conning-tower deck and into heat that seemed to make his red hair curl. Down below, the crewmen paused in their labors and heaved sighs of relief as the depth-gauge needle showed the boat plunging deeper and deeper. There would be a period of shuddering depth charges, but that was strictly routine compared with what they had gone through.

The *Parche* had had quite a run, and so had Commander Ramage. McCrory, Allcorn, Gray, and Plume were all to receive Silver Stars for Gallantry, and the *Parche* and her entire crew a Presidential Unit Citation for extraordinary heroism. And Comdr. L. P. Ramage was to become the first *living* submariner to receive the Congressional Medal of Honor.

As the official citation put it:

17

"The personal daring and outstanding skill displayed by the commanding officer in his series of attacks against a large, heavily escorted enemy convoy . . . is one of the outstanding attacks in the submarine warfare. . . . Only exceptional seamanship, outstanding personal heroism and extreme bravery of *Parche*'s commanding officer saved this submarine from serious damage if not total destruction. . . ."

As Captain Red put it, when interviewed later by a newspaper reporter, "I got mad!"

No group of submariners could discuss undersea war without a mention of Gunther Prien, one of Germany's greatest U-boat aces. His attack on Scapa Flow, fleet anchorage for the British navy, was audacious in the extreme. Winston Churchill said that it must be regarded as a feat of arms. Rear Adm. Dan Gallery, USN, labeled it "the greatest individual feat of arms performed at sea for many years."

Gunther Prien, Kretschmer, and Scheppke were Germany's greatest U-boat heroes. These three commanders sank over 150 Allied ships during their careers as commanding officers.

Suicide Run of *U-47*

FRED WARSHOFSKY

THE German patrols guarding the Kiel Canal on the morning of October 8, 1939, saw nothing unusual in the passage of a slender silhouette through the locks of the canal. U-boats were slipping unobtrusively into the North Sea every day. At this point in the war it was Germany's only entrance to the Atlantic. To the forty-six-man crew of the *U-47* it was, also, merely the start of another war patrol. Only Lt. Gunther Prien, the commanding officer, was aware of the secret mission to which they were assigned. The almost insane venture, if successful, would cripple the British fleet, end the blockade of Germany, and be a feat of arms unequaled in the history of naval warfare.

In spite of the three lookouts and the officer of the deck beside him, Prien felt terribly alone. The stillness was punctuated only by the slapping of the sea and the wind-whipped flutter of the swastika on the mast. Leaning against the forward bulkhead of the tiny bridge, the captain's eyes moved mechanically over the metal deck, awash in the choppy waters. He assessed the capabilities of his boat. Type VII, 740 tons, length 210 feet, top speed 15 knots surfaced, 7 knots submerged. But the major part of his consciousness dwelt on the desperate action for which they were headed.

19

Only a little more than a week before, the *U-47* had been tied to a pier in Kiel. Prien was sitting on the narrow fantail of his boat, enjoying the warm, late fall sunshine when he received an urgent summons to report to Admiral Karl Doenitz. What, he wondered, as he made his way across the dockyard, could the commander of the German U-boat fleet want with him on a Sunday afternoon?

Doenitz' flagship was the submarine tender *Weichsel*. Prien gazed up at the flagship, towering over the four submarines tied to its starboard side. The three-inch gun mounted in the bow looked strangely out of place amidst the tangled jungle of masts, cranes, and booms that sprouted from the tender's decks. He stepped gingerly over the lines and cables that lay flaked out on the dock, skirted the metal bollards over which were looped the heavy manila hawsers that held the 10,000-ton ship firmly to the dockside.

A bosun pipe shrilled as Prien mounted the steeply slanted, ribbed gangplank and stopped on the quarterdeck. He turned and saluted the swastika flying from the stern. Another heel-clicking salute to the officer of the deck and protocol had been satisfied.

Prien followed a goose-stepping messenger down the main deck. Their footsteps rang hollowly as they mounted a metal ladder and turned in on "B" deck. Lining the inboard passageway were a few of the many shops that honeycombed the tender. Machine shops, torpedo, electrical, carpenter—the *Weichsel* was fully equipped to repair and administer to the needs of a fleet of U-boats, in port or at sea.

An orderly snapped to rigid attention as Prien entered Flag Country. The submariner stepped over the high coaming of the watertight door and entered the admiral's cabin.

"Ah, Prien, come in, come in," said Doenitz. His voice was in odd contrast to the high whine of the fresh air ventilators. Doenitz, a lean, angular man in his early fifties, led Prien to his desk in the center of the cabin. He pointed to the sole object on its polished surface—a naval chart. Prien was stunned as he read the upside-down lettering: Scapa Flow. This was a chart of the main anchorage of the British Home Fleet.

The British, referring to the lessons of World War I, considered Scapa Flow of vital importance. It was an excellent harbor, sitting like a bowl in the mountainous Orkney Islands, just off the northern coast of Scotland.

20

Pomona, the largest island, formed, with its sheltering cliffs, the northern and eastern sides of the bowl. The large islands of Hoy, to the southwest, and South Ronaldsay, in the southeast, were the lower half of the bowl. Scattered between these landmasses were the smaller islands of Graemsay, South Walls, Flotta, Burray, and Lamb Holm, which reduced the navigable approaches to the harbor to little more than narrow, twisted channels.

Of Scapa Flow, Winston Churchill had noted in a ministerial conference on September 5:

"In a war with Germany, Scapa Flow is the true strategic point from which the British Navy can control the exits from the North Sea and enforce blockade. . . . Scapa, on account of its greater distance from German air bases, was plainly the best position and had been definitely chosen in the Admiralty war plan."

The defenses of Scapa Flow, both natural and man-made, were formidable. There were but six entrances to the anchorage, three barely navigable by small vessels. Each channel was an intricate and swirling body of water. The violent tides and currents of the channels, often running at speeds of 8 and 10 knots were a natural barrier and one of the most effective of deterrents. It was beyond belief that a submerged submarine could be taken through these turbulent labyrinths and into Scapa Flow.

In addition, modern antisubmarine booms of single-strand net construction had been placed below the surface at each of the three main entrances. The approaches on the east side of the Flow were narrow and tortuous. Obsolete freighters had been filled with cement and sunk in these passages in the last war. These blockships were now reinforced by three recent additions. Gun emplacements, mounting 3.7-inch guns in the surrounding mountains, covered every approach. Three thousand Royal Marines manned the batteries and their 108 searchlights. Destroyers, corvettes, and trawlers patrolled the approaches, while land radar stations aided the surveillance. And minefields in the waters around the Orkneys formed the outer ring of a seemingly impregnable defense.

Prien looked up from the chart at last. He gazed blankly at the bar of sunlight spilling into the cabin through the porthole. Doenitz interrupted his reverie.

"The *Fuehrer*," said the admiral, "wishes to make a U-boat attack

21

on Scapa Flow. To accomplish this, we have devoted a number of aircraft and a U-boat to scouting the area."

Doenitz' plan was exceedingly simple; its execution, enormously difficult.

"This is the Kirk Sound Channel," continued the admiral, his blunt forefinger tracing a dogleg path on the chart. Prien stared at the indicated channel. It was the extreme eastern approach to Scapa Flow, two and a half miles long, running east to west, a wrinkled gooseneck between the mainland and Lamb Holm. The western end of the channel widened like a funnel mouth, spilling into Scapa Flow itself. Sealing off this mouth were three blockships. The chart, however, revealed a very narrow passage between two of the blockships.

"Here," said Doenitz, pointing to the space between the blockships, "a small U-boat might get through. Maneuvering on the surface, and under cover of darkness, it might be done."

Lieutenant Prien drew himself stiffly erect. "I would be honored if the Admiral would consider me to make the attempt."

"Considered . . . *Herr Leutnant,* you have been selected."

Gunther Prien was Doenitz' personal choice and the logical one. He had grown up at sea, serving successively as cabin boy, seaman, and a master in the merchant service. Entering the German navy as an ordinary seaman, he received his commission after completing submarine school. Lt. Werner Hartmann, Prien's commanding officer on the *U-47,* had described him as: ". . . a slim young man of medium height, fair-haired, broad-shouldered, with shrewd and merry eyes."

To his superiors he was known as a dedicated officer. His messmates, however, had another word for it. After once declaring, "I would rather have a month's maneuvers in the Atlantic than any leave," Prien was considered "sea-crazy."

The cry of a lookout quickly brought Prien's mind back to the present. Automatically he bent over the pelorus, swinging it around until the thin hairline of the bearing circle bisected the tiny pall of smoke on the horizon. It could mean only one thing—an enemy convoy. Sublieutenant Endrass, the number one, issued the command that would turn the submarine to an interception course. Prien quickly countermanded the order.

"We're after far bigger game," he told the younger man. "Assemble the men in the forward torpedo room."

The crew of the *U-47* jammed themselves into the small forward compartment of the U-boat. Narrow pipe bunks lined the bulkheads in tiers of three. Overhead swung hammocks, crammed with food and provisions for the patrol. On the deck stood the spare torpedoes in their wheeled trundles. Wedged between the tapered warheads, seated astride the long barrels, the men waited for their captain.

Prien entered and surveyed his crew: the torpedomen, engineers, soundmen, the electricians. Each man had received exhaustive training in his particular specialty. Months of practice had molded them into an efficient team. If anyone had a chance of success, it was the crew of the *U-47*. The captain was terse. "We are going into Scapa Flow," he said.

For an instant they were stunned, quiet. Here was a chance to avenge the two U-boats lost in the unsuccessful attacks made during World War I. And even more significant, Scapa Flow was the scene of the ignominious scuttling of the German Imperial Fleet in 1919. The men broke into cheers.

"We shall be submerging shortly," continued Prien, when the noise subsided. "Get as much rest as you can the next few days. From now on we shall surface only at night."

For four days the *U-47* snaked through the depths, in order to afford no hint of the impending attack. At night they surfaced silently, recharged the batteries, and dumped the weighted burlap sacks of garbage into the sea. Long before the dawn they were again beneath the surface, running toward Scapa Flow.

On the morning of October 13, the slender steel tube of the U-boat's periscope broke through the wavelets, trailing a white feather of foam through the water. In the control room, Prien peered through the angled mirrors and prisms of the periscope. Suddenly he snapped the handles up against the tube.

"Down scope," he ordered. With a whir, the bright cylinder slid down into its well. Prien then pinpointed his position on the chart. They were 20 miles off the Orkney Islands. Just 20 miles east of Scapa Flow and the British fleet.

Tonight would see the culmination of all the careful planning.

Meteorologically, the night had been well chosen. It was the period of the new moon, when the moon is not visible in the heavens. Darkness would be complete and the tides at their most favorable height for navigating the channel.

For fifteen hours the *U-47* lay under 20 fathoms of the North Sea. A barely perceptible rocking was her only motion. The air lay heavy and dank throughout the boat. Cooking odors mingled with the smell of diesel oil, unwashed bodies, and the dank smell of the bilges. And over all, the sweetish scent of Colibri, the cologne all submariners seemed to use to remove the salt and sea spray that crusted their faces.

Only those men necessary to maintain the trim of the boat were on watch. The rest of the crew lay sprawled in their bunks, waiting, waiting. Every four hours the watch was relieved. At 1600 hours wooden planks were placed over the spare torpedoes in the forward compartment. This was now the dinner table for the seamen's mess. After the meal the men returned to their bunks, some to read, others to sleep. From a lower bunk a sailor sqeezed a tinny tune from his concertina. In his cabin, Prien studied the chart Doenitz had given him. The time passed slowly.

At 1900 hours, the hoarse clang of the general alarm rang through the boat. Men rolled out of bunks, jackknifed their bodies through doors and hatches, rushing to action stations. Some men donned headsets, checked out the telephone lines. In the torpedo room, firing circuits were closed, opened, and checked. The men of the *U-47* were at their posts. Prien gave the order to surface.

The inky waters of the North Sea broke into protesting white foam that spilled off the sides of the *U-47* as she reared to the surface. The hatch cover of the control room flew open and Prien sprang to the bridge. He gasped in amazement at the dazzling lights of an aurora borealis that blazed in the night sky.

In his war diary Prien made a terse comment:

"Visibility is shocking. Under the shore everything is dark; high in the sky are the flickering Northern Lights so that the bay surrounded by fairly high mountains is directly illuminated from above. Ships are lying spectrally in the sound like a stage set."

The expected darkness so necessary to the success of the venture was not to be found this night. Perhaps it would be better to postpone the attack? But what guarantee was there that the phenome-

24

non would not be repeated on the following night? No, the attack would have to be made now!

Prien headed the *U-47* for the mouth of the Kirk Sound Channel. The swirling tide was flowing inshore, catching the U-boat from astern and giving it an added impetus. As they entered the channel, Prien slowed the engines. The sluggish craft was harder to handle at reduced speeds, but maneuverability would have to be sacrificed. Their one chance of getting through the twisting channel was to inch their way along. The swift current alone provided more than enough speed.

With consummate skill Prien picked his way up the twisted channel. He inched along, hugging the lee shore of the mainland, hoping its dark bulk would protect them from the eyes of the sentries. To port lay the rocky tip of Lamb Holm. Ahead should be the last obstacle, the cement-filled hulks that stood a subterranean guard at the entrance to Scapa Flow itself. Success or failure depended on their ability to squeeze past those blockships.

With an agonizing scrape of metal on metal, the *U-47* jolted to a halt. Prien cursed under his breath. They had run aground on the blockships. At any second shells would rip the night, tear through the hull of his ship, the bodies of his men. He took a deep breath and raced the engines forward at full speed. With a screech, the U-boat shot forward, off the blockships and into Scapa Flow. It was twenty-seven minutes past midnight, October 14, 1939.

The *U-47* moved southwest, into the heart of Scapa Flow. On the bridge, Prien, Endrass, and the lookouts strained their eyes, searching for the enemy ships. Nothing in sight, and miraculously they were still undetected.

A lookout suddenly hissed a warning. Prien followed the direction of his pointing finger. On the coast road halfway up the mountain, the figure of a man on a bicycle was clearly discernible, pedaling his way home from work. This cursed light, thought Prien. The British must be blind not to have spotted us before this. But where is the fleet? Where are the fat targets? Once again the U-boat commander analyzed the situation, noting in his diary:

"It is disgustingly light! A marvelous view over the whole bay. Southward toward Cava—to starboard—nothing. I come in closer and make out the sentries guarding Hoxa Sound for whom the boat must appear as a target at any second. That would queer the whole pitch, especially as there are no ships discernible to starboard, although otherwise everything is distinguishable for miles. So I decide—nothing to starboard, therefore, before jeopardizing all chances of success some practicable result must be achieved. Accordingly we must turn back and run northward under the coast. . . . There are two battleships lying there and farther inshore destroyers at anchor. No cruisers to be made out. Attack the two big ones. . . ."

The black bow of the *U-47* swung around to the north, its appearance frighteningly ominous in the eerie, flickering blue light. Closer and closer to its target, the U-boat crept. Endrass pressed a stadimeter to his eye, calling off the range as the battleship grew larger in the sight. At 4,000 yards its dark shape bulked over them, the great mast with its spars and rigging pointing a filigreed finger to the heavens; behind it, another silhouette, lying closer inshore.

Prien identified the first as H.M.S. *Royal Oak;* the farther one he took to be *Repulse.* Subsequent intelligence proved him to be only half correct. The second vessel was the obsolescent carrier H.M.S. *Pegasus.*

Prien looked inquiringly at his number one. Endrass nodded his head: *ready to fire.* It was now 0058 hours. Prien pursed his lips, the muscles of his jaw tightened.

"Fire," he snapped in a voice that seemed unnaturally loud in the stillness.

The metallic click of a tube lever echoed throughout the boat, the outer doors opened, and compressed air hissed into the tubes. The *U-47* lurched in recoil as four torpedoes shot from her bow, trailing tiny wakes of phosphorescent bubbles through the water.

Prien leaned forward, eagerly watching the glowing wakes streak toward the target. His open palms slapped the rail in disgust as they continued on past the battleship. Suddenly a shattering explosion ripped the silence, a huge geyser of water shot up into the sky. One of the "eels" had found the mark, slamming into the steel bow of *Royal Oak.*

Incredibly, no alarm was raised. The British had attributed the explosion to internal causes. It was inconceivable to them that a submarine could have penetrated the impregnable fastness of the anchorage. On board the stricken dreadnought, Rear Adm. H. E. C. Blagrove, Second Battle Squadron, rushed forward to determine the cause of the explosion aboard his flagship.

In the unearthly stillness that followed the explosion, Prien came to a quick decision. The *U-47* was still undetected. He would finish the job.

"Reload the tubes," he ordered tersely.

Slowly Prien inched the death-dealing U-boat forward, nearer and nearer to the already crippled battleship. Sweat beaded the captain's forehead. *Why don't they hurry with those torpedoes?* thought Prien.

In the torpedo room, naked to the waist, sailors struggled to reload the tubes. The torpedoes were wheeled forward, the chain hoist was pulled down from the overhead and wrapped around a barrel; then up went an "eel," level with the gaping, empty tube. The torpedomen strained, pushing the long torpedo into the waiting tube.

Twenty-two minutes after the first salvo had been fired, the anxiously awaited report was whispered up to the bridge: *Reloaded.* The *U-47* shuddered once again as it spewed its deadly torpedoes into the night.

This time, the entire salvo ripped into the stricken ship. A terrifying series of explosions shattered the night asunder. *Royal Oak* disappeared behind a cataract of fire, smoke, and water. The proud battleship was literally blown to pieces. Debris flew through the air, falling with a crash into the water, gouging into the surrounding mountains.

Prien watched awestruck as the huge forward turret of the battleship, her great 15-inch guns amazingly still affixed, soared into the sky and then fell with a roaring splash into the Flow.

Of the holocaust he had created, Prien wrote:

"A mighty rumbling, crashing, roaring. First pillars of water, then columns of fire, fragments fly through the air. . . . That wakes the harbor up. Destroyers show lights, W/T signals go out all over the place, cars race along the coastal road. One battleship sunk. All tubes are empty. I decide to withdraw."

The British had indeed awakened, but in a state of hysterical confusion. They were still bewildered as to the nature of their attacker. The air raid alarm went off, piercing the night with its whine. Destroyers raced madly about the anchorage, their searchlights cutting bright swaths of light across the water. In the sheltering mountains, antiaircraft guns pumped flak into the night while searchlights probed the sky with yellow fingers. The British, however, could not

27

conceive that the intruder—that had sunk *Royal Oak* with the loss of Admiral Blagrove and 833 officers and men—was a submarine.

Prien opened the *U-47's* engines wide. The roar of the diesels seemed deafening. Surely they could be heard. He looked astern at their boiling, wide wake, an accusing white arrow pointing right to them. Slow the engines and reduce the wake? But they were barely moving now. Every available ounce of power was needed to buck the fierce current that was now flowing directly on the bow, a giant hand seeking to hold them in the trap. At any moment, the destroyers would seal off every exit. One was bearing down on them at that very instant.

Prien stared at the knifelike bow racing down on them. He could see the masthead light bobbing above the dark bridge as the destroyer cleaved through the water like a rapier. At any second the deadly, orange-red flash of gunfire would dazzle the night.

My God, why didn't they open fire? The destroyer had surely seen them. On its bridge, an Aldis lamp blinked a message. Was he calling the others in for the kill? Its sharp prow loomed up menacingly. Prien could see the creamy bow wave curling back like the lips of a shark. He was going to ram! A collision was inevitable. The destroyer's bull nose would slam into the conning tower, its bow would cut through the U-boat's pressure hull like paper. With an angry gurgle, the sea would rush in and drag them to the bottom.

Miraculously, at the last instant, the Britisher sheered off sharply to port. Prien could clearly see the taut faces of the men on her bridge, completely unaware of the U-boat's presence. In all the noise and confusion, the U-boat, lying low and dark in the water, had been practically invisible. The destroyer raced past, leaving only the sharp knuckle of its wake, a white blur glowing in the dark water.

At last, the entrance to Kirk Sound was ahead. In the constricted passsage, the turbulent current seemed to make a last boiling effort to hold the *U-47* in the trap. Prien slammed the rudder hard over, careening past the southernmost blockship. Lamb Holm was on their starboard beam. Pomona to port. Rocketing heedlessly down the twisting channel, they finally gained the open sea.

Safe at last in the depths, the crew of the *U-47* shouted themselves hoarse, and pounded one another on the back. They had done it . . . penetrated the heavily fortified Scapa Flow, sunk a mighty

British battleship, and gotten out alive. Prien, tired but jubilant, smiled at Endrass. He then retired to his tiny cabin and plotted the course for home.

The psychological effects of Prien's attack were stunning. Winston Churchill, then First Lord of the Admiralty, remarked:

"This episode, which must be regarded as a feat of arms on the part of the German U-boat commander, gave a shock to public opinion. It might well have been politically fatal to any Minister who had been responsible for prewar precautions. Being a newcomer I was immune from such reproaches in these early months. . . . I promised the strictest inquiry."

From the military point of view, the British could do nothing more than offer up their humble thanks that the majority of the fleet had departed Scapa the night before. Had it still been in the Flow, there is little doubt that Prien would have administered a crippling blow that might well have changed the course of the war. Nonetheless, the vital anchorage was lost to the fleet, save as a refueling base for destroyers, for six months. It was not until March 12, 1940, that the defenses had been strengthened sufficiently for the Admiralty to once again risk its capital ships in Scapa Flow.

A Germany wild with joy welcomed its heroes home. Two destroyers escorted the *U-47* into Wilhelmshaven. In the harbor, a hundred ships' whistles, brass bands, and thousands of people roared a noisy salute to Prien and his crew.

Commodore (later Grand Admiral) Doenitz flew down from Kiel to personally congratulate them. With the men of the *U-47* drawn up stiffly at attention on the deck, he awarded Prien the Iron Cross, First Class. Every member of the crew received the Iron Cross, Second Class.

The *Fuehrer*'s personal plane took the heroes to Berlin, where Hitler lunched with them. Afterwards, he awarded the Knight's Cross to Prien—the submarine captain who had made the most daring attack in the history of naval warfare.

I-168 of the Imperial Japanese Navy carried out one of the most successful submarine attacks made by Japan's undersea force. The loss of the Yorktown *at Midway did not affect the great sea battle, for, as the author said, Midway was already lost. With his air cover gone when his four carriers were sunk (one by the U.S. submarine Nautilus), Admiral Yamamoto dared not engage the U.S. Fleet with his powerful cruiser and battleship force, one of the most potentially dangerous surface fleets ever assembled.*

It is interesting to note that I-168 *was ordered to shell Midway Island with its four-inch deck gun until this submarine was joined by the heavy cruisers* Mikuma, Mogami, Suzuya, *and* Kumano. *The I-168's commanding officer said the cruisers' orders were changed; this is true, but they were changed because of the American submarine* Tambor, *whose periscope was sighted by the Japanese as she tried to reach a firing position. The Japanese cruisers made an emergency turn, and* Mogami *rammed* Mikuma. *Admiral Yamamoto ordered the cruisers to retire when he received a report of their damage.*

I Sank the *Yorktown* at Midway

YAHACHI TANABE
with
JOSEPH D. HARRINGTON

THE tension in *I-168's* conning tower had been steadily building up for six and a half hours. In the cramped command post, I stood, palms out, waiting to grip the rising periscope's handles. We were all perspiring heavily. My torpedo petty officer was scanning his switch panel, and a nervous helmsman wiped clammy hands frequently on his pants. Lieutenant (jg) Nakagawa, pencil in hand, mopped his damp brow between looks at the compass and speed indicator. But my gunnery officer, Ensign Watanabe, seemed almost unconcerned. Of the five, his job was by far the simplest. Our submarine was creeping straight toward the crippled American aircraft

30

carrier *Yorktown.* There were no ballistics problems for Watanabe to work out—the range was point-blank, and target speed was nearly zero.

The whine of the periscope's lift motor died away as I sighted through the eyepiece. I had been allowing myself a maximum of five seconds on each sight check and I didn't intend to change the tactic. One quick glance would give me the range, and I could give the order to fire torpedoes.

The periscope stopped. I looked and then stepped back. "Down periscope! Right, 20 degrees rudder! Maintain full silence! Maintain speed of 3 knots!"

My navigator and gunnery officer were astounded. "What has happened, Captain?" they asked. "Aren't we attacking?" They knew we were at that moment so close to *Yorktown* that we could not possibly miss.

"We are going around again," I told them, knowing full well that four, and maybe as many as seven, American destroyers were prowling overhead. "The range is too short! I'm going to open the range and try again. I want to be sure of this kill!"

An odd series of events had put *I-168* where she was on June 6, 1942, deep inside the *Yorktown's* protective circle of American destroyers whose crews were listening for a Japanese submarine. Although I would soon write a last line in that bloody chapter of Japanese history called the Midway Island Battle, the portion I had originally been scheduled to carry out was small indeed. Of the 160-odd ships that gathered from all parts of the Empire to strike at Midway, and the Aleutians, *I-168* had the simplest assignment of all—scouting.

I had missed the war's opening battle. While nearly thirty other submarine commanders were deployed around Oahu, I was plodding our Inland Sea in *RO-59*. My boat trained officers and crews for duty in larger submarines. We knew nothing about the proposed attack on Pearl Harbor, although we did suspect something was afoot because of the heavy radio traffic and many ship movements throughout November, 1941. All ships had been on wartime readiness for weeks. When in port we had a number of surprise drills, during which all hands ashore were ordered quickly back to their ships.

On December 8, 1941, we had such a drill. But when all ships at

Kure reported "manned and ready for sea," we were not given the usual order to secure. Instead, we were told that we were at war with America. Our First Air Fleet had made a very successful attack on the U. S. Fleet at Pearl Harbor, I learned, and we then realized where so many of our first-line units had gone.

Some officers were disappointed at not being in on this battle, but I felt that it would be a long war. Therefore, a highly trained officer like myself, with six special service schools behind him, would eventually see his share of sea action. Nor was I disappointed five months later when my part in the Midway operation was explained to me at Combined Fleet Headquarters. I had meanwhile relieved Lt. Comdr. Otoji Nakamura as commanding officer of *I-168*, in January. Since then we had been exercising in the Inland Sea. *I-168* was designed to make 23 knots on the surface, 8 submerged. She carried ten torpedoes, with four forward tubes and two in the stern. I was satisfied with her.

The Midway-Aleutian force was to be commanded by Adm. Isoroku Yamamoto, who would sail with it in the mighty *Yamato*, the world's biggest warship and our national pride. A total of thirteen submarines were to form the Advance Expeditionary Force, most of them strung out along two lines east of Midway. They were to report any enemy warships coming out of Hawaii to counterattack— then intercept, and sink them. Four carriers, *Akagi*, *Kaga*, *Hiryu*, and *Soryu*, veterans of many successful engagements, were to launch two quick air strikes against Midway, after which 5,000 troops in heavily protected transports would move in and seize the island. This would advance Japan's perimeter well to the east of the homeland. It might even entice the remains of the American fleet out to fight. If so, defeating that fleet would give Japan control of the Pacific Ocean.

I-168's task was to scout to the southward of Midway, and report on as much of the enemy's activities as we could observe. According to the basic plan, we were to see no action at all. We would be near when the troops landed, but by then our job would have been done.

We were the van ship of the entire operation, coming in sight of Kure Island, west of Midway, on May 31, 1942. Part of the overall strategy called for seizing this island, too. It was to be a seaplane and midget submarine base. After radioing a report that nothing appeared to be happening on that island, I proceeded to Midway, and spent the first three days of June making observations there. We would spend daylight hours on periscope watch, on Midway's southern horizon. After dark each night, we moved in within five miles, and continued to watch through powerful binoculars. Our observations made us think that the Americans were expecting imminent attack. I radioed the information that 50 to 100 planes were making landings daily. This meant that American forces on Midway were getting ready to fly extensive patrols, or else were bringing in air protection from Hawaii.

The four carriers of our striking force, although detected at the last, got near enough to launch planes against the island. *I-168* had a front seat, or at least I did, at the day periscope, when 108 of our planes hit the island. Divided into equal numbers of fighters, dive bombers, and torpedo bombers, the last of which operated as level bombers and carried a 1,770-pound bomb each, this force did heavy damage. My crew grew more and more excited as I described the action to them, and a great cheer went up as I described some fuel tanks being blown sky-high.

This portion of the attack appeared to be successful, even though Midway's airplanes had been warned. We saw them take off before ours arrived, and watched them land after that first attack ended. At this point Japan was doing very well. More than 100 of our 108 planes made it safely back to their carriers, while our Zeros shot down or badly damaged two dozen American fighters.

Readers are aware of what happened after that. The Americans counterattacked, with Grumman torpedo bombers, Martin bombers, and Boeing Flying Fortresses, as well as Douglas and Vultee dive bombers. A total of 52 planes attacked our striking force. All were either shot down or driven off, none of them able to do more than get a few machine-gun bullets into one Japanese ship. The American aircraft carriers had slipped into the battle area before our submarine scouting lines had gotten into position. Their planes came next. They sent in an additional 41 planes, 32 of which were shot down. At that point, practically no damage had been done to our side. The fourth of June seemed to be a great day for Japanese arms.

Then the tide of battle turned. While our Zeros were at low level, defending against torpedo bombers, 54 American dive bombers plunged out of the sky against loaded flight decks. They made a

33

shambles of *Kaga, Akagi,* and *Soryu.* No hits were made on *Hiryu.*
She soon got away two strikes. They put three bombs and two torpedoes into USS *Yorktown,* but a return attack by the Americans
hurt *Hiryu* so badly that her crew had no choice but to abandon
and sink her.

By midnight of June 4, the Midway Battle was lost, though we
did not know it yet. Admiral Yamamoto still had hopes of finding
the American ships and sinking them in a surface engagement. It
was only the cautiousness of America's Admiral Spruance that prevented this. Having lost one carrier, Spruance decided it was better
to fight again another day, and he turned his ships eastward after a
short run westward. Comparison of ships' logs after the war showed
that, had he continued westward, his two carriers, eight cruisers,
and fifteen destroyers would have run into a Japanese force that
included seven battleships!

While Yamamoto's main body was steaming eastward, hoping to
catch the American striking force, *I-168* was given orders to close
in on Midway and open fire with her four-inch deck gun. I was to
continue this until joined by the cruisers *Mikuma, Mogami, Suzuya,*
and *Kumano.* These were the world's most powerful heavy cruisers
then. Their forty big guns might easily have smashed Midway's
defenses with a bombardment in the early hours of June 5, paving
the way for an easy landing of the 5,000 troops in the transport
force.

I obeyed orders, taking *I-168* in. We surfaced about 0130 on June
5, but got off only six rounds before a pair of shore searchlights
picked us out. We submerged immediately. Meanwhile, the four
cruisers had their orders changed, and were withdrawing. In the
morning we were sighted by planes and attacked by them, suffering
no damage. We were pursued for a short while by an American ship.

I-168 slipped back onto station as soon as I thought it was safe.
We were supposed to watch the enemy and I intended to do so.

The next time our radio antenna poked above the waves, frightening news came through it. *Soryu* and *Kaga* had gone down the
evening before, *Akagi* and *Hiryu* had followed them not long before
the American planes attacked *I-168.* One of the messages gave *I-168*
a new role to play. Scout planes from Japanese cruisers had sighted
the American aircraft carrier *Yorktown* lying dead in the water

34

about 150 miles northeast of Midway. My orders came through quite clearly: "Submarine *I-168* will locate and destroy the American carrier."

We set off at once, running submerged in daylight hours at the best speed we could make and still nurse our batteries. After dark I ran on the surface, but could not use top speed for fear of missing our target in the blackness. So it was that, at 0530, on June 6, the 12-mm. binoculars of my best-trained lookout picked up *Yorktown*. She was a black shape on the horizon, about 11 miles distant.

It was the easiest intercept a submarine commander ever made. My course had not changed, from beginning to end.

I ordered a dive, a course change to 045 degrees, and then reduced speed to 6 knots, leveling off *I-168* at 90 feet. As we shortened the range, I reduced speed until we were never doing more than 3 knots. At intervals I moved *I-168* up to 60 feet and took sightings. It required only a few course adjustments to set her heading straight for *Yorktown*'s beam.

Our screws were barely turning over, and I hoped they were not giving off enough turbulence for the American ships to detect us. I had sighted one destroyer ahead of the carrier with a towline out to her, and another destroyer nestled close to *Yorktown*'s side. Three more kept station on the side I was approaching, which made me feel certain there must be at least two more on the opposite side. This meant seven of them against one of us.

It never occurred to me to do anything except continue my approach and attack, in spite of the odds. Our intelligence said the American fleet had seven carriers. Two of them, *Ranger* and *Wasp*, were reported in the Atlantic, and we had word that *Saratoga* was on the U. S. west coast. One more, and perhaps two, had been sunk in the Coral Sea Battle a month before. That left the United States with no more than three carriers operating against us, and one of them was dead ahead. Sinking her would mean that the enemy would be left with no more than two to use against us for some time, a vital point now that we had just lost four of our first-line aircraft carriers.

Each time I took a sight, the sun was higher in the sky. *Yorktown* appeared to be making just a little headway. I kept making minor changes of course to keep *I-168* headed at her amidships section.

35

We might get sunk in this action, but before that happened, I meant to do the maximum possible damage to this ship. I wanted my torpedoes to plow into her midsection, not her bow or stern.

In those moments, a lot of faith was being placed by my crew in shrine charms previously given to each *I-168* man by Lt. Gunichi Mochizuki, my chief electrical officer. Mochizuki, a deeply religious man, spent much time at shrines ashore, praying. My crew fervently hoped that his piety had given him some extra influence with the gods. When there was time to turn my thoughts in that direction, so did I.

All *I-168* men limited their movements to the most necessary ones only, fearing to create some sound which the American detectors might pick up. By 1100, I had decided that the enemy equipment was not very sensitive. This gave me confidence as the range shortened; I kept moving in. Suddenly my sound operator reported that the Americans had stopped emitting detection signals. I couldn't understand this but, since it was now nearly noon, I tried to make my voice light and told my crew, "It appears the Americans have interrupted their war for lunch. Now is our chance to strike them good and hard, while they are eating!" There were small jokes made about what to give them for dessert. Shortly thereafter I raised the periscope again.

Abaft my beam, each about 1,000 yards distant, were a pair of American destroyers, one to port, one to starboard. *I-168* had safely pierced the protective screen of escorts; I could now give the order to fire.

Then I took another look. *Yorktown* and her hugging destroyer filled my periscope lens. I was too close! At that moment I estimated my range at 600 yards or less. It was necessary to come around and open up the range.

What I had to do now was try to escape detection by those destroyers above us and get far enough away so that my torpedoes, fired from a 60-foot depth, would have enough running space to stabilize themselves at a 19-foot depth for hitting. Whatever was the reason, enemy sound detectors could no longer be picked up by our equipment; I knew the destroyermen above were not asleep.

I kept *I-168* in a right-hand circle, easing the rudder a little so that I could return to my original track at a point about one mile from *Yorktown*. I didn't dare put up the periscope until the compass showed us back on our original course. So I concentrated instead on a torpedo tactic I wanted to use. Though some submarines in 1942 had Model 95 torpedoes—underwater versions of the very powerful Model 93 "Long Lance" used on surface ships—my torpedoes were an older type. Model 95's had 991-pound warheads, mine had 446-pound ones. So I planned to make two torpedoes into one.

If I followed the usual procedure and fired my four torpedoes with a 2-degree spread, they would cover 6 degrees. But I wanted very badly to deprive the Americans of this carrier. I intended to limit my salvo to a 2-degree spread. I would fire No. 1 and No. 2 first, then send No. 3 and No. 4 in their wakes, on the same courses. That way, I could achieve two large hits instead of four small ones. I could thus deliver all my punch into the carrier's midsection, rather than spread it out along her hull.

When I was back on my approach course, I took another look, and wagged my head at how the destroyers still seemed unaware of us. Either they were poor sailors, had poor equipment, or *I-168* was a charmed vessel. At a range of 1,200 yards, my periscope up, I sent my four torpedoes away as planned. I did not lower the periscope then, either. The wakes of my torpedoes could be seen, so their source could be quickly established. And, if *I-168* was going to die, I at least wanted the satisfaction of seeing whether our fish hit home.

Less than a minute later we heard the explosions. *"Banzai!"* someone shouted. "Go ahead at full speed!" I ordered, then, "Take her down to 200 feet!" My conning tower officers were surprised when I ordered speed cut back to 3 knots a short time afterward, but by that time we were where I wanted to be, directly beneath the enemy carrier. I didn't think she would sink at once, so had no fear of her coming down on us. And one of our torpedoes had run shallow and hit the destroyer alongside *Yorktown*. There would be men in the water. Her destroyers wouldn't risk dropping depth charges for a while, for fear of killing their comrades. Meanwhile, I hoped to creep out of there. I ordered left rudder, and tried to ease away at 3 knots.

My plan didn't work. The American destroyers were on us in no time, dropping depth charges. They had *I-168* pinpointed, and took turns making runs, according to my sound operator. We had torpedoed *Yorktown* at 1330. By 1530, the enemy had dropped sixty depth charges at us, one or two at a time. They were much more sparing with these than they were later in the war, and I took advantage of this by trying to keep an opposite course to whichever destroyer attacked us. The tactic worked a number of times, many depth charges dropping well astern of us as the enemy passed directly overhead.

One of the destroyer captains must have estimated that I was doing this, though. The last depth charge of the two-hour barrage landed just off my bow, putting out all lights, springing small leaks in many places, and causing the danger of chlorine gas forming in my forward battery room.

This was serious. *I-168* had only ten gas masks for a crew of 104 men. But Lieutenant Mochizuki took a small group of men into the forward battery room, closed it behind them to protect the rest of us, and began disconnecting damaged batteries. Before long they had the situation under control, but more trouble was occurring in the bow. Both the outer and inner doors of No. 1 torpedo tube were sprung. *I-168* was partly open to the sea; water was entering the bow section.

We couldn't work on the outer door, of course, so men tried to seal off the inner one, that last depth charge having distorted it. Instead of lying flat in its seal, it bulged into the torpedo room, while water jetted from leaks around its edge. Torpedomen finally plugged the leaks with wedges, however, and everything came under control.

By now we had taken on enough water to weigh the bow down considerably. I ordered all crewmen possible to move aft as a counterweight. This did not remedy the situation, so I employed a tactic used by other Japanese submarines in the war. Every man walked forward again, picked up a sack of rice from our supplies, and carried it aft. This helped considerably, and *I-168* was on an even keel by the time full electric power was restored.

Now we had been operating nearly twelve hours submerged. The destroyers had continued to fire depth charges after 1530, but only sporadically. That sixtieth one had hurt us, and made us bob up from 200 feet to nearly 60 feet. A few more like it, and we might have broached, a perfect target for the searchers. But it seemed as if they were hoarding charges for a final attack, knowing we would have to surface and charge batteries before long.

There were five pistols and ten rifles in *I-168*'s armory. I ordered these issued and told my deck gun crew to stand by near the tower. Sunset was not far off. If we could surface then, and run long enough to charge our batteries, *I-168* might have a chance to reverse the situation, for we still had six torpedoes and five usable tubes left. We might even be able to dive and counterattack, using the darkness to our advantage.

It was still daylight when I ordered "Surface!" There had been a long lull in the firing, and I thought the enemy destroyers might have given up when no sounds could be heard on our detectors. When I got to the open bridge, there was no sign of *Yorktown* on the eastern horizon. I was sure she was somewhere beyond it, sinking, for I had seen the torpedoes hit. Between myself and the horizon, I could see three American destroyers, running in line abreast to the east, on an opposite course from my own. I guessed they were looking for other possible submarines, or else had been summoned back to help with survivors of the carrier.

We were not long on the surface before two of the three ships swung about in pursuit. I estimated their distance at about 11,000 yards. We ran west at 14 knots, the best speed I could make while charging batteries and taking in air. I ordered smoke made, using the heavy black clouds for cover. It helped for a while, and the enemy ships did not appear to be gaining on us very much during the first thirty minutes. I couldn't understand this at all, because of the speed I knew they could make.

When they closed to about 6,500 yards, they opened fire and not long afterward *I-168* was straddled. All a good gunnery officer had to do now was "walk" across me a few times and all would be over.

I can remember the moment of the straddle most vividly. My lookouts began darting quick looks at me, their faces strained and pale. They were anxious to be back in the hull, and diving. I could also detect a high note in the voices below as reports on the progress of the battery charge were called up to me. The men above wanted to dive, though they dared not say so, and the men below wanted to remain surfaced as long as possible while dials and gauges made higher readings. Finally, the enemy silhouettes growing ever larger, I called down, "Do you have enough air and power for short time operations?"

A reluctant "Yes, sir," came up.

"Stand by to dive!" I shouted, and cleared the bridge. I followed all hands into the hatch, ordering *I-168* swung about for a dive into her own smoke. The tactic worked. Both destroyers overran us. They soon had our location fixed again, but dropped only a few charges before breaking off the action and making toward the east at high speed.

I looked at my watch. Only a few minutes until sunset. Whether the enemy ships departed because they feared a night encounter with us, or whether they had no more depth charges, I did not know. In either case, *I-168* was going to get out of this now.

We surfaced a little while after sunset. Assuming that patrol planes from Midway would be seeking us out, we headed north. I hoped they would think I had set a course for Truk, and thus be thrown off the scent. After a few hours, we changed course for Hokkaido, our northernmost island, it then being the nearest to us on a great circle course. *I-168* cruised at her most economical speed, for we were not out of trouble yet. Oil was the Imperial Navy's lifeblood and strictly rationed. *I-168* had been given only enough for cruising to Midway and operating there for a few days. All submarines were supposed to have refueled from captured stores when the island was taken. By practicing severe economies, however, we were able to set Yokosuka, then Kure, as our final destination.

A great crowd greeted our arrival. There were cheers, music, congratulations, and speeches in abundance as we tied up. A special news broadcast had told earlier how *I-168* had torpedoed the carrier *Yorktown*, and that she had sunk the following morning. A special report of the exploit was rendered His Majesty, The Emperor— something done only when the war news was of great magnitude.

I was given command of a new submarine, *I-176*, at once, and granted special permission to hand-pick only men who had factory and machine experience as civilians. This guaranteed me a crack crew.

There were to be other exciting times in the war for me. In *I-176*, I made the first submarine reinforcement of Guadalcanal after the Americans landed there, and with one torpedo knocked out the heavy cruiser *Chester* for a year. Later, after surviving a tenacious attack on *I-176* in the Solomons, I was received in audience by the Emperor himself.

But all I could think of that day at Kure, while being hailed as a hero, was that as yet no news of *Kaga, Akagi, Hiryu,* and *Soryu* had been released to the public. All the Japanese people thought we had scored another Pearl Harbor at Midway. They didn't know that four of our fighting carriers, together with hundreds of Japan's best planes and pilots, were gone forever. My sinking of the USS *Yorktown* was small revenge for that loss.

Lieutenant Fraser, Royal Navy, made one of the classic midget submarine attacks in the history of submarine warfare. Penetrating a harbor guarded by mines, nets, and patrol craft, the plucky crew carried out a well-planned, orderly attack that resulted in the sinking of the Japanese cruiser Takao.

Stalking the *Takao* in Singapore Harbor

COMDR. G. W. KITTREDGE, U.S. NAVY

AT 2300 hours on July 30, 1945, the British submarine *Stygian* came to all stop. Men ran aft along her deck and began to haul in a manila hawser. The midget submarine *XE-3* had just slipped her towline. The attack phase of Operation STRUGGLE was under way.

In the blackness astern of H.M.S. *Stygian,* the *XE-3* looked more like a log floating in the water than a midget submarine—a log or a narrow raft on which the solitary figure of a man was standing. He was Lt. I. E. Fraser of the Royal Navy, commanding officer of the *XE-3.* He had for a crew, Sublieutenant W. J. L. Smith, E.R.A. Charles Reed, and Leading Seaman J. J. Magennis. Four men including the captain had been given the task of penetrating the defenses of Singapore Harbor and blowing up the Japanese cruiser *Takao,* at her moorings some 40 miles away.

The *XE-3* which would attempt to penetrate the defenses of Singapore was the result of much research and experimentation. It did not come into being overnight. There had been many proposals for midget submarines in the Royal Navy. The first was probably an idea for a one-man torpedo put forth by Comdr. G. Herbert, R.N., in 1909. Then there was a design for a three-man midget submarine patented in 1915 by Sir Robert Davis. But none of the proposals were acted on until 1940. That year, Comdr. Cromwell Varley's plan for a midget submarine 50 feet in length with an escape compartment and a crew of three was accepted by the

Admiralty. Strangely enough, when this first midget submarine was constructed, she was given the designation of *X-3*. The final result after four years of design development and operational experience was the *XE-3*, the midget submarine that immobilized the Japanese cruiser *Takao*.

One thing must be remembered about the "XE" craft. They were specifically designed to penetrate harbors and attack ships within those harbors. They were ineffective at sea because they were not the replica of a large submarine made small. They were constructed with a singleness of purpose. They had no superstructure. They carried no torpedoes. The hull was divided into four compartments. The most forward compartment was the battery compartment. Next came the "W and D," or escape compartment, which the diver could flood and then make his exit from the midget through the fore hatch. Aft of "W and D" was the control compartment which contained all the control mechanisms of the craft, steering, trimming, diving controls, and the periscope. The XE class even had a small air-conditioning unit in this compartment. Finally, there was the engine and motor room which also contained the air compressor. The midget had three main ballast tanks plus forward and after trim tank, a compensating tank, and a "negative" or quick diving tank. In addition to the explosive charges which were carried externally in containers on the port and starboard side, the *XE-3* also carried powerful net cutters for use by the diver to cut holes in antisubmarine nets so the *XE-3* could pass through the nets.

All night long the *XE-3* proceeded toward Singapore on the surface while Lieutenant Fraser sat on the casemate and conned her toward Singapore Straits. He deliberately left the marked channel and entered a known minefield to avoid the fixed hydrophones—listening posts which intelligence had told him were in the channel. Along the coast of Johore the *XE-3* sailed, past the island of Pulau Tekong Besar, and finally, a little before dawn, the midget and her crew of four reached the entrance to Singapore Straits.

Lieutenant Fraser strained hard through his large pair of binoculars. There was something up ahead, something big coming down the Straits. He dropped through the after hatch and closed it. The vents to the ballast tanks opened. Air hissed out. All stop. The *XE-3* was heading for the bottom of Singapore Straits until the tanker and the two escorts, which Lieutenant Fraser had sighted up ahead,

43

passed by. There was a metal clank! The four men looked at each other. The noise came from directly underneath them. It sounded again, a noise like a mooring buoy makes when it hits the side of a ship. There could be no mistake this time. It was a mine. The *XE-3* was sitting on top of a Japanese mine! The four men waited. The sound of the heavy, steady, slow beat from the tanker's propeller kept growing louder. Two thin, high-pitched whines could barely be heard above the thump, thump, thump . . . of the tanker. The escorts! The noise of the escorts drew abeam of the *XE-3* and the tanker followed. Minutes passed and gradually the sound of the Japanese propellers became fainter. Fraser ordered the vents to the three main ballast tanks shut and the tanks blown. Would the mine they were sitting on explode? There was complete silence within the hull of the *XE-3* as the little craft left the bottom and headed for the surface. Nothing happened. The *XE-3* continued up the Singapore Straits.

They were getting near now, near to the trawler which tended the antisubmarine net. They were proceeding submerged and Lieutenant Fraser was keeping a constant watch on the periscope. 1030 hours. Trawler ahead. Magennis, get in your suit and aqualung and get ready to leave through the escape compartment. You may have to cut a hole in the net. A hole big enough for the *XE-3* to pass through! Wait! It looks as if the net is open. Slowly, the *XE-3* proceeded past the trawler. Slowly and with periscope housed. Not a ripple must show on the surface above. Nothing must alarm the trawler a few yards abeam. Nothing did. The *XE-3* passed through the opening in the net and continued toward the target. The channel was getting narrower. Narrower, and there was more traffic in the waterway. Small boats. The *XE-3* was approaching the dockyard, up ahead off the port bow. All hands concentrated on their jobs. Fraser, piloting and at the same time searching for the target. Smith, doing the depth keeping, watching the depth gauge and the angle. Reed, steering the courses that Fraser ordered. Only Magennis could relax—as if he could—his job came later, the toughest of all. There she was! The *Takao*? The 13,000-ton, 8-inch-gun cruiser, they had come 40 miles alone to attack.

Lieutenant Fraser watched the Japanese warship through the periscope as the *XE-3* got closer. A liberty launch full of sailors was pulling away from her side. He lowered the periscope and looked at his watch—1400. As good a time as any to attack. He took a last look through the periscope and ordered Reed to steer a course which would head the *XE-3* for the *Takao's* high turret forward, and Smith to increase the depth until the midget was creeping along barely above the mud at the bottom of the channel. Fraser studied the face of his watch. Minutes passed. "All stop!" Magennis headed for the escape compartment. He never made it. The *XE-3* was still sliding along the muddy bottom when she hit the rounded bilge of the cruiser. There was a noise which sounded like an empty steel drum being struck with a sledgehammer, and the midget heeled over. The water under the *Takao* was too shallow. The *XE-3* had wedged herself between the hull of the cruiser and bottom. Fraser backed the midget off and tried again, this time farther aft. For forty minutes he hunted for a place that was deep enough for the *XE-3* to get directly under the *Takao*. Finally, he found one. Magennis flooded the escape compartment and started out.

When he tried to open the hatch, Magennis found it would open only halfway. The *XE-3* had found a place where she could get under the *Takao* all right, but there wasn't any room to spare. The fore hatch, which Magennis had to go through to get out of the midget and place the charges, was prevented from opening more than halfway by the hull of the *Takao* directly above it. Magennis deflated the air sack to his aqualung so he could squeeze through the half-open hatch. He made it. For a half hour, Magennis crawled over the foul hull of the *Takao*, scraping barnacles from her bottom and placing the magnetic-fastened limpet mines. Finally, he finished the job. He placed all six limpets on the *Takao's* hull, spread over a distance of 45 feet. Returning to the *XE-3*, his hands were so cut by barnacles that he had hard work operating the valves to drain the escape compartment.

The limpet mines which Magennis had so carefully positioned on the bottom of the cruiser had been carried in a limpet container on the port side of the *XE-3*. To balance this weight, the midget also carried a similar container on the starboard side, only instead of limpets, the starboard container was filled with a high-explosive charge. As soon as Magennis drained the escape compartment, Lieutenant Fraser ordered both the starboard charge and the empty container dropped. Then, the *XE-3* tried to back out from under the *Takao*. The midget wouldn't move. *XE-3* was stuck. For almost an hour, the crew flooded tanks and blew them, went full ahead and then full astern, rocked the midget and teetered her, trying to shake her loose from the bottom of a cruiser which was due to blow up. Suddenly, without warning, the *XE-3* shot astern. She was completely out of control and porpoised to the surface stern first. Still, the midget's luck held. The Japanese didn't see her. The crew flooded all the tanks and put her on the bottom again. They tried to get a trim and then they realized that the port container, the empty limpet mine container, had not fallen off when they released it together with the main charge. Magennis had to go out again. He had to go out the escape compartment and try to free the empty port limpet container. It took him just seven minutes. Seven minutes to free the bolts which held the container to the hull of the *XE-3* and return to the inside of the midget. Then, the crew of the *XE-3* got the trim, and the midget headed for sea. Toward the open sea she went, past the antisubmarine, past the loop detectors, past the hydrophones and the minefield, and out to deep water where she made her rendezvous with the submarine *Stygian*. At 2130 hours that night, the explosive charges under the *Takao* went off. The charges blew a hole 60 feet by 30 feet in the hull of the Japanese cruiser!

*The story of the U-505 is not only the life story of a German U-boat,
but the life and death story of the German U-boat campaign. U-505
was subjected to air attack, depth charges, sabotage, hedgehogs, a
circular run of its own torpedo and, finally, the extreme disaster of
all, capture by the enemy.*

*U-505 joined her flotilla at Lorient at the height of U-boat suc-
cesses in the Atlantic. She lived on for a nightmarish 404 days to
the end of Admiral Doenitz' dream of bringing the Allies to their
knees.*

404 Days: The War Patrol Life of
German *U-505*

HANS J. DECKER

SINCE 1954 the steps of some two million visitors have clanged on
the deck, ladders, and passageways of a 250-foot monster "moored"
at Chicago's Museum of Science and Industry. This is the German
submarine, *U-505*, captured in a running battle off the Cape Verde
Islands in June, 1944, by USS *Guadalcanal's* hunter-killer group.
The story of her capture is well known. But that was the ending—
the terminus of the life of this U-boat in the service of the German
Kriegsmarine. Where had it all begun? What contributions had the
U-505 made to the German war effort? Her career was unique, and
yet the pattern of her operations was typical of most U-boats. And
that is a story yet to be told.

I remember well how it began, how the *U-505* lived out those
404 days on patrol, and how it ended, because those 404 days also
marked off my war service in the German navy. Fourteen of us
arrived at the main railroad station in Hamburg one warm day in
May, 1941. Our spirits were high. We had finished the three-month
submarine school course at Gotenhafen, in the Baltic, and now had
orders for new construction at the Deutsche Werke shipyard in
Hamburg, where our boat, the *U-505*, was outfitting. By German

47

standards she was a big submarine, a Type IX-C, displacing 1,120 tons; she carried 22 torpedoes, with four tubes forward and two aft; on deck she mounted a 10.5 cm gun; her two M.A.N. diesels and 208 tons of diesel oil could take her 8,100 miles without refueling. In short, she was one of our long-range *front* service boats. Although our formal training days in the classroom, on the drill field, and in our little 250-ton school boats—so small we used to call them *canoes*—were over, the new crew had much to do during the outfitting period. We had to know every nook and cranny and get her ready for action.

By August the whole crew, except the captain, had reported in: *Kapitaenleutnant* Foerster, our chief engineer, *Oberleutnant* Nollau, our exec, *Leutnant* Stolzenburg, the second officer, *Obersteuermann* Reining, *Obermaschinist* Fricke, and all the deck and engineer gang. About the middle of August, 1941, our captain reported aboard. This was *Kapitaenleutnant* Axel-Olaf Loewe, who had just finished a patrol on the *U-74,* as her exec, and now came to us from submarine CO school. His first address to the crew comes back clearly: "Comrades, as commandant of the *U-505,* I have come here to Hamburg in order, with your help, to take our boat to the *front* after our short shakedown and war training maneuvers. It will be a hard life—have no illusions about that—but with a well-disciplined crew, we'll have our successes." On August 26, we hoisted the ensign over our boat for the first time. We were in commission. We had a memorable commissioning party at which the yard commandant, Admiral Wolf, wished us Godspeed and good hunting.

Four days later we backed slowly from the pier at Hamburg, swung our nose toward the mouth of the Elbe and headed for Kiel, in the Baltic, via the Kaiser Wilhelm Canal, for our acceptance tests. October found us at Hela. Then we joined the 25th and later the 27th U-Boat Flotillas off Danzig, where with twelve other new U-boats we engaged in gunnery, torpedo, and tactical exercises. Our surface playmates even gave us our first taste of the realities of war; that is, those of us who were new to the navy. They dropped depth charges—*Wabos,* we called them—one day while we were on a submerged run. So now we knew what they sounded like. But the next time we heard them they wouldn't be dropped for training purposes!

In December, 1941, we returned to the builder's yard at Hamburg for minor repairs and alterations. Before the end of the month, however, Loewe took us to Stettin in the Baltic, where an icebreaker had cut a path for us. There we loaded our stores, oil, and ammo. And what a loading operation it was. . . . There were supplies everywhere: our torpedo tubes loaded with *Aale* (in other navies they call them *fish;* we call them *eels*); the other *Aale,* sixteen of them, lashed in the reload mounts of the forward and after rooms; our sea bags stacked high between the torpedo tubes; boxes, crates, cartons, cans, and what-all piled high in the passageway, behind the diesels, even in the bilges; sacks of potatoes stashed under the chart table in the control room and loaves of bread in hammocks strung up high in both torpedo rooms. We began to wonder if we were a warehouse or a weapon of war. Finally, having made the run back to Kiel, we made ready for sea and the *front*. Our destination? Ah well, as usual, sealed orders to be opened at sea. We were ready and hopeful, because U-boats were having great luck on the hunt.

Around 1300 on January 19, 1942, we began our first patrol. With the crew at maneuvering stations and Loewe at the conn, the deck gang took in the lines. The engine order telegraph jumped—*Halb Fahrt zurueck,* half speed astern, and *U-505* swung slowly away from the pier. This was the first of the 404 days. Down the Kaiser Canal we went and out past Heligoland into the stormy gray water of the North Sea. Before long we heard the crackle of the intercom: *"Hier spricht Kommandant.* Comrades, the Fatherland is now behind us and our first patrol under way. *U-505* has been assigned to the 2nd U-Boat Flotilla at Lorient. Our course to France will be *around* the British Isles. Although we don't have orders to go on the hunt, that doesn't mean we aren't able to sink anything. We'll be hitting heavy weather—a good test for us. But don't let up, because our course takes us through an area under heavy enemy watch. We've had a good start so far; let's keep it that way. *Das ist alles."*

The captain wasn't joking about heavy weather. We ran on the surface all the way, diving only once a day for about two hours to accomplish minor repair work in the quietness beneath the waves. But the trip around Britain (we couldn't go the short way through the Channel because of the minefields) was not entirely uneventful. On January 25 the alarm went off. The bridge watch had spotted a ship in the distant windswept heavy troughs. It was a British destroyer. We didn't dive though, nor did we attack. Nor did he.

49

The weather was just too heavy to line up an attack. And so we continued to the Bay of Biscay, our stomachs in our throats; and not from the excitement of the hunt!

Our escorts, a blockade ship and two motor minesweepers, hove into view on February 3 after our sixteen-day passage and escorted us through the heavily mined waters off Lorient. As we came into the whitecapped harbor on that cold, snowy afternoon, the off watch paraded on the afterdeck. The strains of a military march drifted out toward us as we closed our pier. We could see the faint glint of the band's brass and a rather large group of people from the 2nd Flotilla standing on the snow-tracked quay. In front of the knot of flotilla officers, decked out in navy-blue greatcoats, stood our flotilla chief, *Korvettenkapitaen* Victor Schuetze, a great U-boat ace and holder of the Knight's Cross with Oak Leaves for his exploits while commanding *U-103*. After tying up, Loewe faced the burly Schuetze: "*U-505* reporting as ordered to the 2nd U-Flotilla." "*Heil*, Crew," answered our chief. "*Heil, Herr Kapitaen*," our captain replied for us. Then from dockside came, "We greet the *U-505* and its crew with 'Hurrah, hurrah, hurrah!'" How proud we were that day to receive this official welcome into the flotilla! After all, it was the most famous and successful in the whole U-boat arm. A party ashore followed, at which the staff officers mingled with our officers and crew members alike. And there were toasts—to our boat, to good hunting, and to a safe return to port.

Lorient was quite a place in those days. Sixteen huge concrete bunkers with reinforced roofs 22 feet thick housed the U-boats in port, rehabilitation camps *Prien* and *Lemp* with facilities unparalleled in the German *Wehrmacht* and all just for us and our comrades, a massive command center where the Gray Wolf himself, our Admiral Doenitz, directed his boats to hunt and attack at sea. Lorient was home port for the 2nd and the 10th U-Flotillas. Others were based at St. Nazaire, La Pallice, Brest, and Bordeaux.

At 1000 on February 6 we lined up at division quarters for inspection. Admiral Doenitz himself was the inspecting officer and gave us an official welcome. His final exhortation we never forgot: "*Ran an den Feind, versenken*—go after the enemy and sink him." Our time in port was short now. We loaded stores and fuel again, and about 1500 on February 11 with the free watch paraded on deck, the captain and bridge watch in the flower-bedecked conning

50

tower, and the rest of the crew at maneuvering stations, Loewe called out, "*Leinen los*—cast off." The *U-505* backed from the dimly lit bunker into the ruffled waters of Lorient Harbor. Three sharp hurrahs and the brisk military band march that had echoed in the bunker as we slid out, faded now. We were on our way.

Our escorts for the trip through the minefields and out to the 200-meter line picked us up outside Fort Louis, the last point of land we would see for some time. The captain turned to the exec shortly after this and said, "Nollau, throw the flowers over the side." "Yes, I, too, think that would be best, *Herr Kaleu*," the exec answered. It was a shame really, but according to sea lore at least in German seafaring tradition, it was bad luck to carry flowers. No hexes for us, so over the side they went. When we reached the 200-meter line, our escorts stood by while the *U-505* made a deep practice dive, standard procedure for all boats going out to the *front*. If something went wrong, a boat could return immediately in company of the escort; if all went well, as on this occasion, a boat continued on alone, while the escort signaled a wistful "good hunting."

As *U-505* swung southwest, the engines rumbled louder, turning up flank speed to clear the Bay of Biscay as quickly as possible. These were dangerous waters even in early 1942, because the British had taken special pains to set up surface and air patrols running from Cape Finisterre to Lands End. Here they could catch the greatest concentration of U-boats which had to traverse these restricted waters. Not long after our escorts had disappeared hull down, the intercom blared. Those of us on the engine room watch huddled close to our speaker, trying to catch a few words over the roar of the diesels. "*Hier spricht Kommandant*. We have been ordered on the hunt. *U-505* is going to the West African coast. The waters off Freetown Harbor, where the convoys collect, is our operating area. It won't be easy, though. These are fast ships we're going against. In the meanwhile, eyes open and *ran an den Gegner! Das ist alles*." Freetown? Where was that? We looked at each other and shrugged. And since no one knew, a lively debate followed.

While running through the Biscay, we received special orders to aid one of our sister ships that had received heavy damage in an air attack off Spain. The orders were canceled a little later. The damaged boat managed to work its way into a Spanish port alone. We ran on a more southerly course now. And having cleared the

51

Biscay, we were finally allowed to smoke on the bridge; but only three men at a time because of the imminent danger of enemy attacks. After *U-505* had passed the Azores, though, the captain allowed us a "free bridge" for smoking. In the vicinity of the Canaries, we shut down one engine and ran at half speed in order to conserve fuel. These were lazy days, because we were out of the danger area. But the boat was heating up like a furnace in the daytime. Off watch, we went up on the bridge to get a little relief from the stifling heat down below. The uniform was tropical—no shirts after the first glaze of tan, tropical khaki shorts and pith helmets. *U-505* plowed a thin wake through those clear, light blue waters under the Southern Cross. It was quiet, peaceful, and desolate. The war seemed far off.

Twenty-one days out of Lorient we went to war ourselves. A few minutes after noon on March 5, the engine order telegraph clanged on the diesel not in use, the pointer on half speed. Something was up. Sure enough, the sharp eyes on the bridge—those were infant days for German radar—spotted a smoke plume. Changing course abruptly, we went to flank speed. Then, "*Alarm, tauchen*—dive, dive." In less than half a minute, *U-505* had disappeared from the surface. We were now at battle stations at standard periscope depth, 20 meters. "Make ready one and two," came the order from the conning tower. Dials on our torpedo data computer whirled—courses, range, speed, and gyro angle, all worked out in the matter of seconds. Silence, and then, "Fire one, fire two." The boat lurched ever so slightly as two deadly black torpedoes whished out of the tubes in the forward room. We all began to count. " . . . 15, 16, 17, 18, 19." Then it came—a soft boom, that was all; one hit. The klaxon went off. "*Auftauchen*, surface." There close aboard lay the stricken British freighter, *Benmohr*, of 6,000 tons, her stern already high out of water, as she began the long death glide and slipped under the surface amid a spray of boiling water. We were jubilant; our first action, our first success. We took it as a good omen and hoped for more like it.

That was not long in coming. Just twenty-four hours later, another smoke plume drifted to windward over the horizon, not far away. We dove. "Make ready three and four." "*Los*, fire." Again, we took up the count, " . . . 7, 8, 9." And this time a sharp explosion, whose shock wave rocked us gently a few moments later. Immediately,

Loewe ordered, "Battle stations, surface." Up we went. The sea was empty except for a huge oil slick that was spreading in an ever widening circle. Suddenly, the diving alarm went off—"*Tauchen,* plane to starboard." We dove to 80 meters, but nothing happened. Loewe entered in our logbook, "—March 6, 1942. English tanker, 8,000 tons, name unknown. Target exploded and sank in 25 seconds." Not a bad start for a new ship: two days, two hits, two ships.

U-505 now came into her assigned operating area, north of Liberia, and cruised slowly back and forth off the port of Freetown. But we spotted nothing, absolutely nothing. Loewe took us farther southward. Even here, there was not a sign of a ship. This went on for three weeks. It was disgruntling to say the least. As we turned north again on April 1, we crossed the equator. What a day we had! No, we didn't attack any ships; we did have our Neptune celebration. These festivities helped take our minds off the monotony, the turn of bad luck we seemed to be having on the hunt, and the oppressive equatorial heat. It seemed a good omen for the future.

Just two days later, on April 3, we got a contact. A five-hour chase began to get into an attack position. About 2200 we went to battle stations, torpedo, on the surface. The captain gave the conn to Nollau, the exec, who directed the attack. *"Torpedo los."* We counted off the seconds—" . . . 11, 12, 13 . . . 17, 18, 19. . . ." It was *only* 1,000 yards to the target. "21, 22, 23, 24. . . ." Missed. Two shots, no hits. Now the captain took over the new approach and fired twice more. We waited in vain for the explosion. *"Auf Artillerie Gefechtsstation!"* roared Loewe; "gun stations." Our deck gun had barely gotten off the first rounds, when suddenly our target, the American freighter, *West Irmo,* broke in half and disappeared within two minutes. Fearful of attack because the ship had sent out an SOS, we dove and cleared the area.

Just as *U-505* had had two consecutive days of good hunting a month before, so the next day our lookouts again sighted smoke. Two hours later there was no more smoke plume and no more ship. Two torpedoes had finished off a 6,000-ton Dutchman, *Alphacca.* Ringing up flank speed, the captain moved *U-505* north. Now we returned to the quadrant off Freetown, hopeful that our fortune had turned for the better. In the next two weeks we didn't sight so much as a fishing boat! *U-505* had now been at sea for over seventy days. The strain was beginning to show. Looking at the same faces day in and day out, listening to the same stories grown old after the first few weeks, and now the dismal luck on the hunt had frayed nerves here and there. It showed in little ways—sharpened remarks and glum faces lined with fatigue that resulted from stifling, sleepless days and nights. Then on April 21 Loewe announced, "Beginning today we start our trip home." Thereafter, the sun came up on the starboard side.

Soon only six men at a time were allowed on the bridge during their off-watch hours; then none, because we were threading our way past the Azores and up the Spanish coast. Then the dread Biscay, fortunately rather tame for us—only two depth charges dropped in the distance. The last few days out we found plenty to do. Razors and scissors appeared, as we trimmed up the long hair and beards we had let grow since leaving port. We cleaned up our dress uniforms for the formal inspection on arrival. Some engineers made four little flags, each signifying a ship sunk, that would fly from the periscope shears when *U-505* entered port.

On the morning of May 7 escorts met us off the entrance to the minefields. That afternoon *U-505* stood into Lorient after eighty-four days at sea, four ships totaling 26,000 tons to our credit. We were conscious of those little flags whipping in the wind above the conning tower. Many people were on the pier; the station band and members of our own flotilla, all in summer uniforms, gave us the customary, though enthusiastic, three cheers. Then came congratulations from Flotilla Chief Schuetze and others, reports, interrogations by the submarine intelligence service, our mail and leave papers. Perhaps the proudest moment came when we each received the official U-boat badge. Now we were U-boat veterans.

The month passed quickly; leave in Germany, then preparing for our next trip: stores, oil, and ammo. On June 7, 1942, we began our third voyage. Again, there was the band and members of the 2nd Flotilla lining the passageway in the bunker, the hurrahs, and the flowers on the conning tower. Our escorts picked us up off Port Louis and left us after our practice deep dive. We ran at flank speed that night on the surface and by morning had covered a good part of the Biscay. At dawn we dove, and Loewe opened our orders. "Men, our third operation has commenced. We've been ordered to the Caribbean, and so we have a long run to make across the Atlantic. I don't have to tell you, the bridge will have to keep an

54

especially sharp lookout. We'll be crossing many commerce routes. In fact, the success of our trip will depend on how well our bridge watch does its job. The antisubmarine techniques of our enemy are improving from day to day. Therefore I require continuous improvement of my crew. *Das ist alles*." We were pleased with our assignment. Some boats in our flotilla had had excellent luck in the Caribbean recently, firing all torpedoes and returning to Lorient flying a half dozen or more little flags.

The remainder of our trip out of the Biscay was underwater. The enemy was at work in the area, because we heard distant explosions. Six days later we were off the Azores and veered off on a more westerly course. The trip across was peaceful and warm. We sighted nothing but flying fish, porpoises, and albatrosses. Again we had a free bridge. Finally, on June 28 a telltale smoke plume appeared over the horizon. This one looked easy, because *U-505* lay right across the ship's course. Something went wrong with the navigating calculations, though, for we ended up in a seven-hour-long chase at high speed. After diving, Loewe got a good setup and fired twice. Both *Aale* ran true and hot. The victim was a 6,900-ton, *Robin Hood*-type American merchantman.

The next day, another black smudge on the horizon set us on the chase again. When we dove, the captain took the conn, stationing himself at the attack periscope. "Make ready tubes one through four." "One through four ready, sir," reported the forward room. "Fire one, fire two." As usual we counted off the seconds. Two muffled explosions reached our ears, and smiles broke out on our faces. "Surface, gun stations." Air hissed into the ballast tanks, and *U-505* nosed up quickly. After several rounds, Loewe called, "Cease fire; the off-watch may come on deck." This was the first chance many had had to see just what we were doing. There lay a big American freighter with a heavy list to port, decks crowded with aircraft. She rolled over on her side and slipped under. Two lifeboats, full of men, came close aboard. We asked if they needed water or provisions, gave them the course to the nearest land, and then cleared to the north. We had sunk the brand new freighter, *Thomas McKean*, 7,400 tons, on her maiden voyage. Our spirits were high—two ships in two days. *U-505* now set course into the Caribbean via Mona Passage, which we entered on July 3, and took station off Colon. A month before, one boat had picked off nine ships in five days. Could we not expect a little luck for ourselves, too?

For sixteen days we moved slowly back and forth off Colon. Not a thing in sight; the sea was empty. Finally, in disgust Loewe took the boat south to the coast of Venezuela. Here, on July 21 we underwent our first ordeal. A plane almost caught us on the surface and dropped two bombs before we had even 50 meters of water over us. U-505 suffered no damage, however, and no further attack came. On July 27 the bridge watch caught sight of sails. The captain set up an intercept course. When the windjammer hove into view, Loewe tried to see what colors she was flying, but couldn't make out anything. Then, we went to gun stations. "Fire a shot over her bow, so we can find out who she is," the captain called out to Stolzenburg, the gunnery officer. The first shot went through her mainmast, and now mast and canvas hung drunkenly half in the water. Still unable to see what nationality she was, Loewe made a quick decision. "Sink that thing, but quick, Stolzenburg." Two shots finished her off. Her name was the *Roma*, about 400 tons. Only much later did we discover she belonged to neutral Colombia.

Now Loewe took sick, and many of his duties fell to Nollau, our exec. A few days later we started home, very low on diesel oil. When this was reported to Lorient, the submarine operational staff set up a rendezvous with our "milch cows" 500 miles south of Bermuda. These supply U-boats were either Type IX, like ourselves, or Type XIV boats modified to carry extra loads of oil, provisions, and torpedoes. Acting as movable bases, they allowed U-boats to stay on station for longer periods of time. Their value is obvious. Meeting one as scheduled, we took on 12 tons of diesel fuel and supplies. U-505 continued on course for Lorient across an empty sea, save for a herd of whales that passed close aboard.

On August 25 our escorts appeared and brought us in. From the periscopes flew three little flags, representing 14,700 tons of shipping. Thus closed our first year in service. Our record: seven ships, 40,700 tons. The band and the flotilla staff were on the dock to greet us, as usual. But Lorient was showing signs of change. The port was coming under heavier and heavier bombing attacks. There was noticeable damage here and there. The U-boat bunkers were intact, though. The enemy never did destroy them in the whole course of the war. Also on the way in we had seen a strange red buoy in the channel. We inquired about this. It seems that a U-boat, coming home after a 110-day patrol off Madagascar, struck a mine under the eyes of the band and members of the flotilla waiting to welcome it. There were only two survivors. The enemy had mined the channel the night before.

U-505 was in port for five weeks. We had leave while the ship underwent repairs and alterations. They increased our fuel oil capacity and installed the new "Metox" device for air warning. Also, we lost our captain, who went on sick leave, and the popular exec, Nollau, who got command of a new U-boat. Peter Zschech, exec on the famous *U-124*, became our new skipper; his friend, *Oberleutnant* Tilo Bode, exec. We all felt we were in good hands. On October 4 we cleared Lorient again, with the usual send-off by the band and flotilla representatives. It was louder and more tumultuous than ever before, though. Zschech was very popular in the flotilla, and his friends and ours made quite a gathering along the gangways of the bunker. On the way out two strange things happened. All the off watch was ordered topside with life jackets and told to kneel on the deck. This, it was explained, was in case we hit a mine going out. Mine explosions, it seemed, had a nasty way of driving the legs vertically up into the body. And Zschech wouldn't throw over the flowers that lined the leading edge of the bridge. We wondered about that.

After our practice dive, we left our escorts and moved southwest. The Biscay crossing was uneventful, our Metox giving us adequate warning when planes approached. On October 6 we received orders from headquarters: destination Trinidad, there to concentrate on tankers which made up in convoy in that area. During the four-week trip to our quadrant, our new captain ran many drills. We were a good crew, and he seemed satisfied with our performance. On station the first week in November we patrolled the mouth of the Orinoco River. The heat was frightful. Moreover, we didn't see a thing. Then on the seventh, the bridge spotted a light, and started a night surface attack. "Battle stations, torpedo," shouted Zschech. "*Los*"; a single torpedo streaked toward the target. The ship disintegrated. We discovered neither name nor nationality, but Zschech thought her about 5,000 tons. From that day on we were under nearly constant air search, diving many times at night to escape detection, and once heard one depth charge go off. On the ninth,

57

we spotted another ship and attacked at night. Zschech tried twice. Four *Aale*, no hits! And then the ship got away from us. We looked at each other in wonder. This had never happened before. The flowers, those damn flowers. . . .

The next day, November 10, *U-505* stood east of Trinidad. It was one of those days so common in the tropics: not a cloud in the sky, the water like blue crystal glass and a scorching sun, so hot that we thought we were inside a baking oven. We were lolling along the surface. The excellent Zeiss binoculars of the bridge watch swept through the assigned sectors. Nothing could be seen other than the shimmering sea. It was a tiring chore. The early afternoon sun was in the watch officer's sector. *Leutnant* Stolzenburg raised his glasses directly into the sun. There was a faint shimmer up there. Was it a bird, perhaps? Suddenly, the watch heard the drone. That bird had two engines! "Alarm, dive, dive." It was too late. We hadn't even started down when a series of rapid shocks and explosions that literally raised us off our feet hit our boat. The lights went out, and the engine room watch stared unbelievingly as a jet of water sprayed against the port diesel. We were hurt. "Surface, surface; all hands put on life jackets. Flank speed on the diesels." The whole port propulsion unit was out of commission, however; the exhaust valve frozen closed.

The captain went immediately to the bridge. There lay Stolzenburg. He had been hit in the back. Zschech looked around. What a mess. It looked as if a bulldozer had run over the deck—twisted steel, crumpled sheet metal, broken and twisted pipelines. Sections of the false hull had disappeared. The 37-mm. antiaircraft cannon had been blown overboard. And from behind the ship streamed an ever widening ribbon of a thick, black substance. The bombs had split open our fuel tanks. A nice track that was. Zschech looked hurriedly upward. Why no further attack? We were defenseless; unable to dive. Then he saw why. Off to starboard drifted part of the plane's fuselage, and on our own foredeck lay a section of a bright yellow wing. Below, we discovered that the after bulkhead of the engine room had buckled; the water had come from our freshwater cooling pipes, smashed in by a huge dent in the pressure hull over the port diesel. The captain wished he hadn't kept those flowers now!

The next five days were a nightmare. *U-505* ran slowly eastward on one engine, while we struggled to repair some of the damage. We had to get the boat into diving condition, or we would never make it. Work had scarcely begun before the bridge watch shouted, "Aircraft to starboard." There we were, helpless, not a gun in operation. Zschech ordered a change of course, placing our stern to the enemy to present the smallest silhouette. It worked, and we breathed deeply as the plane disappeared. Work began in earnest. The engine gang started repairs on the broken water pipes, while the deck crew cleared off as much as they could topside. They found the pressure lockers for our two spare torpedoes split wide open. They jettisoned the torpedoes. We flanged over the hole in the pressure hull but couldn't get the other diesel working. Four days after the attack we tried a test dive. Our lives depended upon its success.

It was deathly still in the boat when we shut down the diesels. No one moved. "*Fluten*—flood," said Zschech to our chief engineer, who stood at the hydraulic manifold. We heard clearly the snap of the vent levers as they hit the stops, and the gurgle of water entering into the tanks as they flooded. Twenty meters—"all clear"; 30 meters—"all clear"; 40, 45. We were sinking too rapidly. A loud clank sounded from the engine room. The pressure hull had buckled inward a few centimeters more. "We can only dive to 30 meters with any safety," announced the captain. But we could dive! We had a chance!

Now the job centered on keeping the boat running and getting the radio into operation. We needed fuel, we needed help. That night our radioman got his set working, and by rigging a jury antenna got off a message to Admiral Doenitz' headquarters telling our plight and needs. Almost immediately came the reply. A supply submarine, *U-462*, would meet us off the Cape Verde Islands; fifteen days later we rendezvoused. The crew of *U-462* couldn't believe their eyes. They had never seen a boat so heavily damaged. Taking on oil and spare parts for the port diesel, we transferred the wounded Stolzenburg to *U-462* which carried a doctor. Then, we parted company. That day, November 28, we got the port diesel back on the line.

Late that afternoon we had a contact. In spite of our condition Zschech decided to attack on the surface. In two attacks we fired four torpedoes. No hits. The target slipped away both times. The next night another turned up. We fired again but overshot, and the ship disappeared in a burst of speed. The next night we spotted a ship aft, just where the others had come up from. A ghost ship, we began to think. This time Zschech made a long shot. We waited and counted the seconds. A thud came all right, but against our own hull! A circular run or perhaps the enemy? All stations reported, "Clear." It had been a dud. "That's enough for this trip!" exclaimed our captain. We ran through the entire length of the Biscay submerged.

Off Lorient we had to wait for the escorts. Another boat, flying six victory flags from her periscopes, was waiting ahead of us. We thought ruefully of the single little pennant that fluttered above our bridge. Coming into Lorient, we saw a large crowd on the dock, their eyes on the boat ahead with its six pennants. We were bows on, and only one little flag flew over us. When U-505 began to swing in alongside the pier, exposing the entire damaged length of our hull to those ashore, they came running up the pier to check our number and to inspect our damage. The whole 2nd Flotilla staff came aboard, and after Zschech made his report, we all heard the flotilla engineer remark, "This is the most damaged boat ever to come back under its own power." We liked to think of it differently: the only boat with such damage that ever made it home. . . . And we received a special commendation from Admiral Doenitz.

The U-505 was due for a long stay in port this time: seven months. Work began while we were on leave. The yard put on a whole new conning tower that fairly bristled with antiaircraft guns. Enemy aircraft had become the U-boat arm's gravest antagonist. In addition, they put in 36 square meters of new pressure hull to replace the damaged section, and took off our deck gun. There would be no more surface artillery attacks. All this took a long time.

U-505 was ready for sea again in late June. During those months in port the enemy made heavy air raids on Lorient in an attempt to knock out the 2nd and 10th U-Flotillas and the U-boat pens. They did not succeed. But we heard of their luck in another area of activity. During April, May, and June ninety of our boats failed to return. This was getting to be a suicidal trade we were following. Also, there was no more fanfare when leaving port. The boats slipped out with the least possible commotion at night. And only six men stayed below to man the controls on the way out. The rest of them were on deck in life jackets. This was the way we went out under escort on June 30, 1943. At the 200-meter line we made our test dive, a real experiment for us. At 150 meters everything was fine. At 180, however, a sharp snap rang through the hull. We surfaced immediately, and found that the main induction in the conning tower had burst. We had to go back to port.

Zschech was anxious to get out on the hunt. He didn't have to wait long, because on July 3, *U-505* started out again. This time all went well on the deep dive, and we started a full power run out of the Biscay, now known to all German submariners as *"Der Selbstmordstrecke—the suicide stretch."* All night long the Metox device showed aircraft nearby, but no attacks came. Zschech ran us on the surface from dusk to dawn to make use of every minute of full power, so that we could get out into the Atlantic. Five days out of Lorient, on July 8, we were off Cape Finisterre at twilight, and getting ready to surface. The captain ordered us to periscope depth, rode it up from the deck, and took a look. "Quick, take us down to 60 meters. There are three destroyers up there not a mile away, and headed straight for this spot." *U-505* had scarcely reached the ordered depth when the first depth charges went off. "One hundred and twenty meters. Emergency lights," Zschech murmured. Four more charges went off nearby. Then silence; we hoped they had lost us. But we couldn't shake them. In desperation we fired a torpedo, but missed. This went on for thirty-six hours before we finally lost them. When we surfaced, we found out why they had stayed with us so long. On the surface in our wake was an oil slick. The first attack had opened one of our tanks. They had simply followed the slick.

Again we returned to port. We couldn't repair the leaking tank, and besides the attack had jammed our radio gear. We spent the next two weeks getting repairs. Also a new exec, *Oberleutnant* Meyer, a new second officer, and a doctor reported aboard for duty. Before we started out again on August 1, we heard tragic news. Enemy destroyers had sunk *U-124*, with her great captain, Knight's Cross holder Johan Mohr, and his entire crew. Zschech, who knew them all, seemed pretty glum on the way out. On the deep dive, water came in. Back to port again went the *U-505*. This time the engineers found a hollow sweat seam in the pressure hull, and even some seams calked with oakum. Was this sabotage? Most of the yard workers were Frenchmen. . . . We were getting rather disturbed at this point, but it wasn't over yet. When we went out on August 15, the valve on the main induction buckled and filled the line with seawater. Again we returned to the bunker for repairs. On August 22 we hadn't gone very far before one of the enginemen discovered *sugar* in the lube oil. That was sabotage! During the week *U-505* was back in Lorient, a new piece of aircraft detection gear, the *Naxos* device, was installed. It didn't work on our sixth attempt to break out on August 30, and we came in again. By this time we felt we were riding a jinx ship. Anyway, none of us thought our chances for getting through the Biscay very good at all. The crew was never lower in morale. Obviously, the tide of war had turned against us.

On September 18 we tried again. This time all went well on the dive. The escort with the yard engineers who came out with us went back in without us. Our hopes began to soar. Zschech kept us at flank speed on the surface all that night, and no one disturbed us. Perhaps our luck was changing. Everything was fine until the night of the twentieth, when a cylinder in the port diesel froze up tight. We scoffed a little, however, because we had enough spare parts to repair it ourselves. On September 23 we cleared the Biscay. But that same night our luck ran out. The trim pump, one of the most important pieces of machinery in a submarine, broke down. There were no spares on board. There was nothing else to do except run the gauntlet back to Lorient. We made it safely, and no one seemed particularly surprised to see us again when *U-505* came into the bunker on September 28.

It was October 18 before we got under way again. The dive went well at the 200-meter line, and five days later the boat had cleared the Biscay. Zschech now opened our orders: the Caribbean again. During the next few days came training exercises. After all, we had been in port for over ten months. On October 26 in the vicinity of the Azores, *P-505* turned westward. That evening, while changing the watch at 1800, we heard something unbelievable: the unmistakable sound of fast-turning propellers close aboard. We didn't have much time to think about how it could happen. When we were at just 50 meters the depth charges began exploding. They were right on. We thought this was the end, as glass crashed around us and the boat shook and shuddered violently. Six more charges went off close aboard. We were in total darkness this time, and were thrown violently about with the gyrations of the boat. Still, no reports of a ruptured hull came. Then many of us heard a sharp crack, like a pistol shot, from the vicinity of the control room.

There came an announcement over the intercom. "First officer speaking. The captain is dead. We are going to 150 meters. Silent running. *Das ist alles.*" Zschech dead? We hardly had time to think about it, because as we started down, a new attack commenced and continued without letup for the next two hours. Finally they lost us. We were all pretty shaky by that time. Again the intercom crackled. "To all stations. This is the exec. The captain is dead. I am assuming command. We're going home. . . ." What had happened? We soon found out. Zschech, thinking it was all over, had committed suicide. We had indeed lost the man who had led us for more than a year. But there was more to think about just then; we couldn't surface because we could still hear explosions in the distance. The air was so foul now that Meyer had carbon dioxide absorbent spread in the compartments. Finally at 0400, after the sound man reported no trace of our attackers, we surfaced. How sweet that fresh air smelled! We buried *Kapitaenleutnant* Peter Zschech at sea before daybreak. It wasn't much of a service for the man who had held such great hopes for us and our boat—and we for him. Meyer then rang up flank speed to get out of this deadly area. October 26, 1943, was a day we would long remember, but not with relish.

We sent in a message reporting the death of our captain to both Admiral Doenitz and our new flotilla chief, Commander Ernst Kals. Both requested further information. They received no word, however, because murderous days followed. Attack after attack befell us; we had an oil leak, and the enemy picked up our track easily. At headquarters they reported us lost. Somehow we managed to make it. We radioed for escorts finally, and came into Lorient on November 7. There were only a few people on the dock to greet us. The flotilla chief welcomed us home and praised our work in getting the boat and ourselves in safely. We were the only boat in. The 2nd and 10th Flotillas had suffered heavy losses. Most of the supply U-boats had been lost, too. For all of that, however, the 2nd Flotilla was still the most successful in the entire U-boat arm with 5 million tons of shipping to its credit.

U-505 underwent repairs for the next month and a half. We were ready for sea again on Christmas Day, after a disillusioning leave— things were very bad at home what with the bombings and the bad reports from the front. We had a new captain to take us out, *Ober-leutnant* Harald Lange. The escorts left us after the test dive. There-after we ran submerged. On December 28 we got orders for a special rescue mission nearby. British light cruisers had sunk our torpedo boat, *T-25*. We were going to try to rescue the crew. That night in the middle of the Biscay, our small searchlight playing over the water, we rescued thirty-two crew members and the captain of the *T-25*. We arrived with them at Brest on January 2, 1944. There, as luck would have it, we burned up our port maneuvering controller and the armature of the port main motor. This called for a major repair job in one of the Brest U-boat bunkers. At the end of January the repairs were completed. Our exec, Meyer, took the conn when we moved over to another bunker. On the way in, we rammed the side of the bunker. Then on our way into the repair bunker for in-spection, we crashed again, ripping off the after-port diving plane and bending the port shaft. This meant another month in port. We had given up hope of getting out long before this, though.

Late at night on March 16, 1944, *U-505* backed slowly out of the bunker. Only a few people saw us off. There was no band, there were no hurrahs, and no flowers this time. In fact, many of us won-dered whether we would ever again see those bright stars that shone overhead on our way out. The trip down the Biscay surprised us. Our radar worked very well and gave us plenty of warning at night in time to dive. We were out into the open sea on the twenty-first. Two days later we met the incoming *U-154* and passed the new radio code on to her. We learned from her that *U-66* had had great luck a few days earlier just to the south, sinking five freighters in no time at all. The area was now under heavy search. We heard, too, for the first time of the new Allied hunter-killer groups, com-posed of small aircraft carriers and destroyers, that were raising havoc with our U-boats.

We then continued south. Our destination was the area off the port of Monrovia, Liberia. We had been there before some two years earlier. We spotted a light soon after our arrival on station. Upon investigation, however, it turned out to be a lighthouse in Monrovia Harbor. That was the closest approximation to a target we saw in the next month and a half. The hex was still with us. It was maddening. Absolutely nothing turned up. We were down on oil near the end of May and having some real battery trouble. We started home on the twenty-seventh. What a dismal trip; not a sinking to our credit. On June 2 Lange tried to stay on the surface longer than usual to bring the batteries up to full charge. We had had so many air alarms at night in recent weeks that the batteries were in bad shape because of the abbreviated charging periods. We simply could not stay under water for any length of time.

On June 4 the captain decided to take us close to the Verde Islands in order to shorten the homeward trip. A few minutes after 1100 that morning, as we glided slowly northward running submerged, something strange happened. From over our heads came a scraping sound, as if someone were dragging a cable along the deck above. It stopped, then started again. This was bewildering. We didn't have too long to think about it, however, because within moments our sound man picked up propeller noises; not just one set, but three. They were all around us. "Battle stations, torpedo," cried Lange. "Periscope depth, and make it slow, Chief; maybe we're in the middle of a convoy." We never got there, because Lange ordered us deep as a series of little sharp explosions rocked us. These were not depth charges, but the dreaded "hedgehogs," little rocket-like devices, which, exploding only on contact as they did, had spelled death for many of our U-boats. At 50 meters we were hit with another attack. These were depth charges this time, and they were close aboard. U-505 shuddered violently, the lights went out, and amid the din we heard the most dreaded of noises to submariners: water rushing in. Sure enough, someone shouted, "Ruptured hull in the control room." And in the engine room the flashlights played on streams of oil and water from broken pipelines.

We were really in trouble now; more trouble than most of us knew. The boat was out of control and now down over 230 meters. The pressure hull wouldn't take that very long. "Take us up, take us up before it's too late," cried Lange. That was the last organized order for the U-505. Someone blew the ballast tanks, and the next thing we knew we were on the surface. Those of us still below could hear the sounds of gunfire, and then a voice shouting from somewhere, "Raus schnell—Abandon ship, we're sinking!" In the confusion and near-panic that followed as the last of us scrambled up the conning tower ladder to the bridge, no one thought of opening the vents to sink the boat. Some water was coming in all right, and Holdenreid, one of our engineers, tried unsuccessfully to open a sea valve that would have sent *U-505* to the bottom posthaste. Actually, at that moment most of us were concerned with the unknown future that lay ahead in those next few moments. What awaited us? A bullet from the plane that was strafing? Going down with our boat? Capture?

As the last of us emerged into the bright sunlight at about 1125, we could plainly see what had happened. There standing close into our position—our changing position because the motors had been left running and we were moving in a wide circle at seven knots—there stood our protagonists: an aircraft carrier and five destroyer escorts. A hunter-killer group! Small wonder that we hadn't been able to get away. All the crew, with the exception of poor Fischer, our radio-man, who had been killed in the strafing, were now in the water. We expected *U-505* to slide beneath the waves at any moment, because the afterdeck was already awash. But to our amazement she just continued on, running in a slow circle. Other matters occupied our minds for the moment, however. The American destroyers began picking us up. When we looked again we were thunderstruck to see a large American ensign flying from the conning tower of *U-505* and noticed a small whaleboat standing by her. Not only had they captured us, but our boat as well! And that afternoon *U-505* stood on a course for Bermuda at the end of a towline behind the USS *Guadalcanal*. That's her story. It was the 404th day of her war patrol career, an unlucky day for her. But then *U-505* was a hard-luck ship. . . .

The capture of the U-505 was the first United States capture of a foreign man-of-war in battle on the high seas since June, 1815, when the American sloop of war Peacock *boarded and seized the British brigantine H.M.S.* Nautilus *near Singapore. The capture of the U-505 made naval history.*

From the Allied point of view, the exploit is even more dramatic than the 404 days of the German U-boat's life. The capturing force, a hunter-killer group consisting of a small aircraft carrier with accompanying destroyer escorts, spelled the doom of Hitler's great U-boat armada.

The Capture of *U-505*

DAN GALLERY, REAR ADMIRAL, U.S. NAVY (RET.)

At 1121½ on June 4, 1944, 150 miles west of Cape Blanco, French West Africa, the *U-505* heaved itself up from the depths and broke surface 700 yards from the *Chatelain*—white water pouring off its rusty black sides. Our quarry was at bay.

When a cornered sub first breaks surface, you can never be sure whether the enemy came up to abandon ship and scuttle or to fire a spread of torpedoes and try to take some of our ships to the bottom with him. *Pillsbury, Jenks,* and *Chatelain* cut loose with all the guns they had, and for about two minutes, 50-caliber slugs and 20- and 40-mm. explosive bullets hammered into the conning tower and tore up the ocean around it. Our fighter planes sent streams of hot metal ricocheting across her decks. Fortunately, all the three-inch stuff we fired missed, as did a torpedo fired by *Chatelain* when she thought the sub was swinging around to bring her own torpedo tubes to bear.

As the sub ran in a tight circle to the right, small crouching figures popped out of the conning tower and plunged overboard. While these men were leaping for their lives amid our hail of bullets, I broadcast to the Task Group, "I want to capture that bastard, if possible."

After about fifty or so men had gone overboard, Commander Hall, at 1126, ordered, "Cease firing"—and the ancient cry, "Away all boarding parties," boomed out over modern loudspeakers for the first time since 1815. The *Pillsbury's* party, led by Lt. (jg) Albert David, had already scrambled into their motor whaleboat and the boat plopped into the water and took off after the sub, which was still circling to the right at 5 or 6 knots. As that tiny whaleboat took off after the circling black monster, I wouldn't have blamed those men in the boat for hoping that maybe they wouldn't catch her. The Nantucket sleigh ride they might get if they did overhaul her would top anything in Moby Dick! But cutting inside the circle, the gallant band in the boat drew up alongside the runaway U-boat and leaped from the plunging whaleboat to the heaving, slippery deck. As the first one hit the deck with the whaleboat's bowline, it looked for all the world like a cowboy roping a wild horse. I grabbed the TBS and broadcast, "Heigho Silver—ride'm cowboy!"—not a very salty exhortation but readily understood by all hands.

On deck was a dead man lying facedown with his head alongside the open conning tower hatch, the only man killed on either side in this action. He was Hans Fischer, one of the plank owners of the *U-505* who had been aboard since commissioning. David and his boys now had a wild bull by the tail and couldn't let go. They were in charge of the topside of this submarine, but God only knew who was down below or what nefarious work they were doing. Somebody had to go below and find out.

No one in that boarding party had ever set foot on a submarine of any kind before—to say nothing of a runaway German sub. Anyone who ventured down that conning tower hatch might be greeted by a blast of gunfire from below! Even if abandoned, the ship might blow up or sink at any moment. That sewer-like opening in the bridge leading down under the seas looked like a one-way street to Davy Jones's locker for everyone in the boarding party.

Lieutenant David, Arthur K. Knispel, and Stanley E. Wdowiak jammed all these ideas into unused corners of their minds and plunged down the hatch (David told me later that on the way down he found out exactly how Jonah felt on his way down into the belly of the whale).

They hit the floor plates at the bottom of the ladder ready to fight it out with anyone left aboard. But the enemy had fled for their lives and were now all in the water watching the death struggle of their stricken boat. My boys were all alone on board a runaway enemy ship with machinery humming all around them, surrounded by a bewildering array of pipes, valves, levers, and instruments with German labels on them. They felt the throbbing of the screws still driving the ship ahead and heard an ominous gurgle of water coming in somewhere nearby. This was a new version of the "Flying Dutchman," even more eerie than the old sailing ship with all sails drawing and not a soul on board.

But the submarine was all theirs. All theirs, that is, if they didn't touch the wrong valve or lever in the semidarkness of the emergency lights and blow up or sink the boat. David yelled up to the boys on deck to tumble down and lend a hand while he, Knispel, and Wdowiak ran forward for the radio room to get the code books. They smashed open a couple of lockers, found the books, and immediately passed them up on deck, so we would have something to show for our efforts in case we still lost the boat.

Some readers, knowing that all naval code books have lead covers to make them sink, will ask why didn't the Germans throw these code books overboard? But why throw a code book overboard from a submarine which you are abandoning in over a thousand fathoms of water, thinking she will be on the bottom in another couple of minutes? *Nothing* had gone overboard except the crew, and we now had in our possession one U-boat, complete with spare parts and all charts, codes, and operating instructions from Admiral Doenitz. It would be the greatest intelligence windfall of the war, if David could keep her afloat.

It seemed doubtful that he could, because the sub was now in practically neutral buoyancy, was riding about 10 degrees down by the stern, and was settling deeper all the time.

One of the first to plunge down the hatch in response to David's call from below was Zenon B. Lukosius. As soon as "Luke" hit the floor plates he heard running water. Heading for the sound, he ducked around behind the main periscope well and found a stream of water 6 inches in diameter gushing into the bilges from an open sea chest. By the grace of God the cover for this chest had not fallen down into the bilges where we wouldn't have been able to find it, but was lying on the floor plates. Luke grabbed it, slapped it back in place, set up on the butterfly nuts, and checked the inrush of water. By this time

69

the boat was threatening to upend like the *U-515* any minute. If she had, she would have taken the whole boarding party with her. Luke got his little chore done just in the nick of time. Another minute might have been too late.

Luke told me later that while he was jamming that cover back in place, he was too busy to be scared. But when he tore his Mae West life jacket on a sharp projection in the conning tower, that really shook him—because he didn't know how to swim.

The sub was now so low in the water that the swells breaking across the nearly submerged U-boat were beginning to wash down the conning tower hatch. David ordered the man left on deck to close the hatch while he and his men continued their work below. The main electric motors were still running and driving the sub in a circle at about 6 knots.

Meantime, I had reversed course, got back to the scene of action and sent over a whaleboat with Comdr. Earl Trosino and a group of our "experts" in it. They arrived aboard the sub literally "with a bang." A swell picked up their boat and deposited it bodily on the deck of the sub, breaking the boat's back and spilling the occupants on deck unceremoniously. This blow from above caused some concern even to David and his stouthearted lads below, who at this time were engaged in ripping electric wires off things which they thought were demolition charges.

When Trosino and his crew scrambled up to the bridge, they couldn't get the conning tower hatch open. It was stuck as if fastened from the inside, a partial vacuum inside the boat holding it down so the boys couldn't budge it. The circling U-boat was constantly passing Germans in their rubber boats and Mae Wests, so Trosino's boys grabbed one, hauled him aboard, and asked him how to open the hatch. The German showed them a little valve which let air into the pressure hull, equalizing the pressures inside and out, and enabled them to get the hatch open.

"Thanks Bud," said Trosino, and shoved him overboard again.

Trosino then scrambled down the hatch and took over command from David in the same spot where *Oberleutnant* Meyer had assumed command after Zschech ran out on him. No other U-boat ever had so many changes of command under fantastically improbable circumstances!

I cannot speak too highly of the job that Trosino did in keeping that sub afloat. He too had never been aboard a submarine before. But he had spent most of his life at sea as a chief engineer in Sun Oil tankers. He is the kind of an engineer who can walk into any marine plant, whether it is installed in the *Queen Mary* or a German U-boat, take a quick look around the engine room and be ready to put the blast on any dumb cluck who touches the wrong valve at the wrong time.

He spent the next couple of hours fighting to keep the sub's head above water. It was touch and go whether he would succeed or not and they had to keep that conning tower hatch closed. A lot of the time Trosino was down in the bilges under the floor plates tracing out pipelines. Had the sub taken a sudden lurch and upended herself, as it was quite probable she would—Earl wouldn't have had any chance whatever to get out. I recommended him for a Navy Cross when we got back to Norfolk. All he got was a Legion of Merit. He did this job in the wrong ocean! But that Legion of Merit is worth more than some of the Navy Crosses they were handing out in the Pacific at this time.

Trosino got the right valves closed and didn't open any of the hundreds of wrong ones. While he was doing this, Gunner Burr went through the boat looking for demolition charges. Our intelligence reports told us we would find fourteen 5-pound TNT charges placed against the hull, several in each compartment. We had no information on their exact location or how the firing mechanism worked. Gunner Burr found and disarmed thirteen while Trosino was bilge diving. They found the fourteenth in Bermuda three weeks later! The Germans had been so sure when they abandoned ship that this sub was on the way to the bottom within minutes, that they hadn't set the firing devices! This information is worth only a raised eyebrow now, but when Burr, Trosino, David, and their boys were aboard that first day, the knowledge that there was an unlocated demolition charge raised the hackles along all their spines.

Shortly after Trosino got aboard, the *Pillsbury* came alongside to pass salvage pumps over and take the sub in tow. Her skipper didn't allow for the fact that submarines have large flippers sticking out from the bow underwater on both sides. The sub's port bow flipper cut a long underwater slice in the *Pillsbury*'s thin plates as she came alongside, flooding two main compartments and making it necessary for the DE to back off and fight to keep herself afloat.

71

Trosino reported that as long as the sub had headway, she rode about 10 degrees down by the stern. But when he slowed her down, she lost the lift of her stern diving planes, settled to a steeper angle, and submerged the conning tower hatch. The *Pillsbury* reported a DE couldn't do the towing job, so I headed over to take her in tow myself. As we drew near, Trosino pulled the switches and stopped the sub.

Working fast, we laid our stern practically alongside the nose of the sub, threw over a heaving line with a messenger line and an inch-and-a-quarter wire towline bent on. As the lads on the heaving, slippery deck of the sub were struggling to secure the towline, with four loaded bow torpedo tubes of the submarine practically nuzzling my after end, I said a fervent prayer. "Dear Lord, I've got a bunch of inquisitive lads nosing around below in that sub—please don't let any of them monkey with the firing switch!"

When the towline was secured, we eased ahead, took a strain, and got under way again with the U.S. colors proudly flying over the swastika on a boathook planted in a voice tube on the *U-505*'s bridge. As we gathered speed the stern came up and they could open the hatch again. I cracked off an urgent top-secret dispatch to CinCLant and Cominch, "Request immediate assistance to tow captured submarine *U-505*." That dispatch really shook the staff duty officers back home. At first they didn't believe it and demanded a recheck on the decoding—but lost no time getting necessary action under way in the improbable event that it was true.

Some submarines have had the reputation of being bad-luck boats.
Herr Oberleutnant Erich Topp must have thought his U-boat was
one. Or was it because he sailed on the thirteenth day of the month?

The Red Devil Boat

HARALD BUSCH

FEW U-boat crews can have functioned better as a team or held together more proudly, despite the fact that the pick were lost to a promotion course after every patrol, than the men of the *U-57*, one of the small, "coastal" U-boats of 300 tons.

This particular boat bore as an emblem on her conning tower two prancing demons, each bearing aloft a burning torch. They had been put there by her first commander, and it was from them that the *U-57* acquired her nickname, the Red Devil Boat. But that was later, when she had become famous. When Erich Topp took over the command, the *U-57* was merely the *U-57*.

On Friday, October 13, 1940, the *U-57* was due to set off on patrol, the first under her new commander. Friday the thirteenth! So Erich Topp, mindful of the old superstition, sailed, instead, on the Thursday—sailed right across the harbor to berth again on the opposite side, finished taking on stores, and put quietly out to sea on the morrow before Fate had a chance to look around. Or so he hoped.

They were still in the North Sea, a thoroughly murky day, when a drifting mine lurched up, groped and ground its way horribly along the casing, then freed itself and drifted harmlessly away. (According to international agreement, mines that broke loose from their moorings were supposed to unprime themselves automatically, but you never could tell!)

In Norway, Topp replenished his supply of diesel fuel, then set off to search in earnest for the enemy. Hardly had he left Korsfjord, when, on the silk-smooth sea, one of the lookouts on the bridge spotted the bubble tracks of two compressed-air torpedoes making straight for the boat. "Hard-a-starboard!" roared the officer of the watch. "Full ahead together!"

Scrambling to the bridge, Topp was just in time to see the tracks go streaking past the boat, a spreading salvo from a British competitor. An attempt to pursue and outmaneuver the enemy submarine failed, owing to a breakdown in the hydrophone gear, and the *U-57* was forced to disengage.

The first part of the patrol lasted for five days, and within that time the small number of torpedoes which the coastal-type U-boat could accommodate had all been expended. Topp had sunk a lone steamer bound for Britain with a cargo of timber, and another ship traveling in convoy and loaded with ammunition. Despite the continued strike of the hydrophones, he had evaded the subsequent rain of depth charges from the escorting destroyers and earned a congratulatory signal from Doenitz: *Well done,* U-57! *Keep it up!*

A quick call at Bergen to replenish supplies and the *U-57* again put to sea. In foggy weather off the northwest coast of Scotland, a gigantic convoy was sighted, but at the decisive moment the new engineer officer failed to put on the trim and Topp had to let the convoy go; it was the biggest he was ever to set eyes on during the whole of his career at sea.

In the North Channel, at the entrance to the Irish Sea, the *U-57* came upon a 5,000-tonner, sinking her after an arduous pursuit and at the fourth attempt. Then, spotted too late for the U-boat to submerge, a plane dropped bombs, fortunately all duds.

Next, Topp put into Lorient, again to replenish supplies. On the way north the boat was again attacked by aircraft, holed fifteen times by machine-gun fire, but nobody hurt. The plane dropped one bomb, which failed to explode.

In barely a week, the boat was again in the North Channel, and for ten days the little ship battled through heavy seas amid unrelenting storm. For ten days, no sight or sound but the lash and splutter of the spray, the sky's lament, and the wind's despair. The hydrophones had been temporarily repaired, but on the very first day of the storm they broke down again, depriving the commander of his only contact with the outside world when the U-boat was submerged.

Eleventh day out of Lorient—sea moderated to Force 6—steamer in sight and coming closer. The boat bounds about like a tennis ball. She simply cannot be held at periscope depth for a daylight underwater attack, slicing down, lifting again, the bow, even the conning tower, breaking surface, then slumping once more into the trough of the waves, till finally she finds herself following close in the wake of the escaping enemy. His name is just discernible on the stern: *Ceramic*. But in such seas pursuit is impossible. He's lucky. Sixteen thousand tons—what a haul! Already, in the first world war, the *Ceramic* had survived three separate U-boat attacks; some ships are like that.

Thirteenth day. With daylight a plane comes diving suddenly out of low cloud. This time the bombs are distinctly unpleasant and the boat is badly shaken. One of the diesels is ripped off its bed, the camshaft snaps, and most of the instruments are smashed. The boat dives—luckily the pressure hull is still watertight—and being close to the land and in shallow water, she can be laid on the bottom.

While the damage is being repaired, the commander discusses the situation with his officers. The chief engineer, as the man responsible for the technical functioning of the boat, urges emphatically that they should return to base. Diesels are beyond repair and the rest of the damage can at best only be patched up in the hope that somehow they will manage to struggle home. Reichenbach, the young officer of the watch, suggests, on the other hand, that they cannot possibly return home without firing a single torpedo, the whole set untouched and intact.

The commander agrees. But how can they get within range of a target with a crippled boat, maximum surface speed 9 knots? The only chance would seem to be to station themselves at some point which the enemy more or less has to pass and wait there until something happens. Only the chief objects. Resolved: return to North Channel.

So at nightfall, the *U-57* goes pounding laboriously back into the narrows, passing several destroyers unobserved. On shore, the navigational beacons are still burning. In the first world war the Irish Sea had been one of the U-boats' principal hunting grounds, but today, with their carefully thought-up system of air and sea patrols, with their anti-U-boat defense operating with such smooth efficiency, the British believe they can afford to let their lights burn on. U-boats? So far inside home waters? Impossible! Thanks to the

75

beacons, the *U-57* can be navigated with marvelous precision.

Cautiously, Topp worms his way on the surface deeper and deeper into the lion's den, still unobserved, past all the enemy patrols. How long can this last, he wonders?

A few hours after entering the narrows, he sights an approaching convoy. Fortunately, the moon is hidden. With grim perseverance, Topp maneuvers into position and, as he runs out, fires the whole salvo of three torpedoes. Soon after the first has left the tube, the U-boat is sighted by a destroyer on the starboard flank of the convoy. To fire his second shot Topp has to head straight toward a second destroyer, stationed between the lines of ships. The track gives him away, and immediately both destroyers turn and make toward him at high speed.

Meanwhile, the first torpedo strikes its target with a heavy explosion, then the second. But before Topp can have his third shot, there is still some way to go. At last the sights come on and he hears the officers of the watch: *"Rohr drei—Llosss!"* feels the boat falter as the third torpedo leaves its tube, then: "Control room, control room! DIVE—DIVE—DIVE!" The main vents are opened, while on the bridge the night-sight is unrigged at top speed and vanishes through the hatch with the lookouts. Last to leave, the commander scrambles down, clamping the cover behind him.

Now, as the boat is diving (in only 25 fathoms), the third explosion is heard, again a direct hit. Suddenly a broad stream of water curves into the bow compartment and, seconds later, the nose of the boat bumps heavily on the bottom. Hell!

"Blow for'ard!" Quick! Away from the diving position before the destroyers are on us! Off the bottom, come on, up! What's happened? Changeover valve still open! Now, as the bow lifts, the stern immediately slumps to the bottom and sticks there. Too much water in the boat, three tons in excess of her diving weight.

The roar of the depth charges begins.

"Belay bilge pumps!" All machinery is stopped so as not to give away the position to the enemy sound detectors and the boat lies quietly on the bottom. Meanwhile the seawater that has broken in is collected, bucketful by bucketful, and dispersed evenly throughout the bilges. In this way perhaps the trim can be restored.

And still the depth charges go on erupting, all around the boat, far too close for comfort. The damage mounts. After every explosion, new leaks in the hull are reported, spurts and drips of water are everywhere.

Now the lights go out and in the darkness animal fear grows, feeding on uncertainty. Topp forces himself to speak in an easy, conversational tone, asks a question, makes some light remark, shielding the men from the truth, for the truth is that their fate stands poised upon the razor's edge. . . .

The depth-charging goes on for the rest of that night, and the following day, and yet another night. Every half hour one of the pursuers glides past overhead, unloading as he goes.

Then, each time, there is a pause—the minutes tick by—no sound—and still no sound—can it be? Here they come again, the destroyer's propellers. Oh, God, they're stopping; the Asidic's pinpointing the boat—they're starting again—look out, here it comes. . . .

A cavernous roar, then another, till it seems incredible that the boat can still survive. Perhaps she is lying in a fold of the seabed, sheltered from the full impact of the blast—is that the explanation?

Another hour passes. The air is foul, the air-conditioning plant no longer functioning. Topp sends the crew to their bunks. Each man is given a potash cartridge with a tube on the end to breathe through. He puts the tube in his mouth, and as he breathes through it, the potash removes the carbon dioxide. The commander and the officer of the watch sit huddled on the chart cupboard in the control room, the only place they can find, for normally the whole crew are never off duty at the same time and bunks are provided for only half the complement.

The remainder lie huddled in their blankets on the bare steel plates of the deck, some of them in inches of water, and the commander has to pick his way carefully over them as he goes the rounds every half hour with a flashlight to make sure that the tubes have not slipped out of the mouths of those who are sleeping.

Yes, some of these youngsters are actually asleep, free as they are of responsibility, free of the necessary imaginative power to foresee—and foretaste—the end. Toward midday, they begin to feel hungry. No hot food can be prepared, so sandwiches are made and passed around. They eat them lying down.

Meanwhile, the air in the U-boat is getting more and more oppressive, can be breathed only in quick, shallow gasps. All around, the explosions continue. Then again there is a pause, till propellers can be

77

heard revolving very slowly, directly overhead. Suddenly, there is a jerk, the bow is lifted up, falls back again. The men jump, wild-eyed, to their feet, then freeze, motionless, listening. . . .

There! Hear it? Something scratching along the hull. "Sweep wires!" whispers the second officer. The commander nods, thinks: Must keep calm, the flick of an eyelash, and there'll be panic—

The wires scour over the casing, then fall away astern. The sound of the propellers grows softer as the destroyer drags for the U-boat farther off. Every now and then a depth charge is dropped. The hull rocks and creaks, dribbling everywhere. The last bilge pump goes out of action. If the fuel bunkers were not contained inside the pressure hull in this type of boat, some diesel oil would long ago have risen to the surface, marking the spot for the kill.

The hours creep on, the darkness within the boat spreading to the world outside. Here in the hull, night has long since fallen, suffocating, clammy, the stagnant horror of the tomb. . . .

The pursuers draw away and once more silence returns. This time, after more than 200 depth charges, they seem satisfied that their work is done.

22:30 All quiet, manage to get bilge pump working. Hope to surface at 23.00.
22:40 Still quiet.
22:50 More depth charges. Will have to wait now till midnight, at least.
24:00 Blow all tanks. Rise off the bottom.

The U-boat surfaces, the conning tower hatch flies open and sharp, clean air pours into starved lungs. Sea Force 6, pitch-black night: couldn't be better. One destroyer, one other vessel stopped and just discernible dead astern, but lying so low in the water, the submarine is harder for them to see and they do not stir. "Group down, slow ahead together." Almost noiseless at this speed, the electric motors are engaged instead of the diesel and the U-boat creeps off on the surface, her presence still undetected.

Both compasses are out of action and there is not a star in the sky. No chance of a navigational fix. But the storm is still blowing, probably from the northwest, as it was forty-eight hours ago when last observed. It means taking a chance, but as the only hope of escaping from the deathtrap of the North Channel, Topp sets a course head on into the seas.

Meanwhile every available man gets feverishly to work repairing the internal damage. By daylight the magnetic compass is clear again and Topp can verify his position. He finds that his guess was right and that now, at last, the *U-57* is upon the open seas.

The boat dives so that the two torpedoes remaining in reserve can be loaded into the tubes, then surfaces again. Aircraft on the starboard bow! And in the distance, smoke clouds—a convoy. Down quickly, then full speed toward it, just in time to catch a lone ship straggling at the tail. Topp runs out to attack, firing two torpedoes. The tanker explodes in a ball of fire, dense clouds of pitchy smoke surging upward and spreading to the farthest corners of the sea.

A special U-boat chaser pursues them, dropping depth charges, eighty of them, with twice the explosive power of the earlier ones. The boat rattles and shakes, suffering yet further damage. But this time she can descend to a greater depth and, though slowly, continue to move, making good her escape.

At last the hunt is broken off and all is quiet again. Now Topp can lay his brave boat on the ocean bed, allow his crew and himself to rest, wonderfully peaceful at last, and undisturbed.

A monster gala banquet is prepared (to become traditional in the Red Devil Boat, after the last fish has been fired and the bow has turned toward home). All the delicacies that the kitchen and cellar can produce—and the U-boats didn't do badly for food—are brought out to be recklessly consumed. A bill of fare is passed around so that, informally and according to rank, as the official phrase would have it, each member of the crew can mark off the items of his choice.

Then the great meal is served, Topp sitting with his men, now no longer the new commander on his first patrol, but the Old Man, the man to be trusted, the man who now sits, numb with exhaustion, after leading them through mortal perils to the performance of memorable deeds.

But the *U-57*, the boat that sailed on Friday the thirteenth, was not yet at the end of her voyage.

On the following day, the one diesel still in action developed clutch trouble. The reversing clutch was adapted for forward drive and the boat went hobbling on. Each day she was attacked several more times by aircraft, each time diving to avoid the bombs and bullets. At last, despite the vigilance of the lookouts, an enemy plane was sighted too late and a hail of bullets descended on the boat as she was submerging to safety. She was holed in ten places, but no one was injured.

So she continued homeward, till one evening just after nightfall she drew in toward Brunsbüttel. Signal contact was established with the movement staff at the lock on the seaward side of the canal and the all clear was given to come in. The lock gates opened. A Norwegian steamer began to move out as the U-boat started to move in. "Red-to-Red!" Then suddenly the steamer's green light was visible, too. With his stern still inside the lock in slack water and his bow just through the gates in a tide running at 4 knots, the Norwegian was carried, helpless, across the bows of the U-boat. "Full astern!" roared Topp—too late.

There was a grinding shock as the U-boat was rammed. A split second's frozen horror, then Topp ordered all hands overboard. The conning tower swung wildly, brushing the side of the steamer at deck level, then the boat went down. In fifteen seconds, she had disappeared.

In that short time, the majority of the men managed to scramble overboard, to be seized immediately by the fast-flowing tide and carried out to sea. After an all-night search, the survivors were finally brought together.

One of them had been in the W/T office when the boat went down. When she came to rest on the bottom, he had found himself standing, with his head in an air bubble. Several times he tried to find his way, swimming underwater, to the conning tower hatch in the adjacent compartment, returning after each attempt to the air bubble to regain his breath. At the eighth attempt he succeeded, only to find the hatch blocked by the bodies of his messmates, drowned while trying to open it. He clawed them aside, groped for the hatch cover, forced it open, and so came to the surface. He was found that night, unconscious and totally exhausted, having been washed ashore by the tide.

With the gray December daylight, he insisted on joining his comrades of the U-57 to report to the commander. Just as they were, some still huddled in blankets, they strung out, a sad, exhausted group. The senior took a pace forward, then spoke slowly, his voice reduced to a whisper from the salt water that had scored his throat: "Herr—*Oberleutnant*. Crew present, sir, all but six. I've been asked—

80

to ask you, sir—we'd all like to put in to stay together as a crew, sir—and may we have you, sir, please, as our commander—"

It seemed as if Topp were about to speak, but no sound came from his lips. Like most of his crew, he was bareheaded, so he could not salute. They saw him stand there motionless, for a moment, in the icy wind, then turn and walk slowly away.

Great Britain has had, by far, the largest amount of operational experience with the submarines of other nations. During World War II, her 9th Flotilla, based at Dundee, consisted of the Polish Wilk, Dutch O-14, Free French Minerve and Rubis, and Norwegian Uredd. These were only a few of the submarines serving the Allied cause during this war. From time to time, Greek, Italian, and Russian submarines also operated with Allied forces.

One of the most difficult situations to arise among the combined Allied submarine forces was the split in loyalty among the French submarines. Many French boats fought long and well for the Allies, while others lined up with the Vichy forces to fight for the Axis.

The Russian submarines, by the very secrecy of their operations, proved difficult allies. It was sometimes nearly impossible for other allied boats to coordinate with them. By Allied standards, Russian submarines were sadly deficient in communications, navigation, and the techniques of the approach. A British mission to the Russian submarine base at Polyarnoe, on Kola Inlet, soon rectified some of the worst problems. When two British submarines were sent to augment and coordinate the movements of the Russian squadron, results were achieved. While the British admired the courage of the Russian officers and crews, they were appalled by the filthy living conditions aboard the submarines, and the tight control exercised over the men by the Russian political commissars. The commissars hampered cooperation in every way. Russian submarines were, however, usually "smart," and their sailors were the pick of the Russian navy.

American submarine experience during World War II was limited generally to overhauling Russian, Dutch, and French submarines, and coordinating patrols with Dutch and British boats in the Far East. In one small way American submarines had a connection with the Free Polish Force; an S-boat loaned by the United States government to the British, prior to America's entry into the war, was later turned over to the Poles and renamed Jastryab. Unfortunately, British surface forces later sank her through an operational error.

While it would be impossible to mention all the submarines that served the Allied cause, special note should be made of the Free French Rubis, O-21, O-16, and K-14 of the Dutch navy, the Greek Triton, and the Polish Sokol and Orzel.

Orzel escaped from Poland when Germany invaded that country. She was forcibly interned by Estonia, but fought clear of the harbor of Tallin in a hail of bullets. After many harrowing experiences,

*she outwitted a massive German attempt to destroy her and finally
made port in Great Britain.*

*Individual commanders of some of the smaller submarine forces
during World War II performed some remarkable exploits. The
story of Commander "Bob" Karnicki, commander of the Polish submarine* Sokol, *clearly demonstrates that skill and courage cannot be
measured by the size of the force.*

The Fighting Pole

RICHARD BAXTER

IT IS possible that, so far as Polish submarines are concerned, the
record of *Sokol* will rank as one of the most outstanding of the war.

The *Sokol* was added to the Polish navy in 1941. One of her first
operational voyages, which involved a sea trip of several weeks,
gave her the chance to sink a large Italian destroyer of the *Alvieri*
class in the Bay of Navarino, damage a second destroyer, sink an
auxiliary cruiser and four transports, and damage six other enemy
craft.

In addition to all this good work, *Sokol*, after getting entangled in
an antisubmarine net, managed to clear herself while actually undergoing depth-charging, and proceeded to rescue British airmen who
had been brought down off the coast of Libya.

The *Sokol* was commanded by Commander "Bob" Karnicki, a tall,
muscular Pole in his early thirties, whose one passion in life had
been submarine operations. He was first lieutenant on board the
Wilk when she forced her way from the Baltic.

Shortly after being commissioned, the *Sokol* was sent out to cruise
in the Bay of Biscay, with the idea of operating against enemy transports and supply ships creeping along the coast of France. Three
times she sailed to Brest to lie in wait for the *Scharnhorst* and the
Gneisenau, when reports were received to the effect that they intended to make a dash for the Atlantic with the idea of preying upon
shipping.

Sokol, however, was destined to gain fame in the Mediterranean.

An urgent call went out for more submarines to operate against the Italians and against the German transports which were taking troops and supplies to North Africa. At top speed *Sokol* made for Gibraltar, and there received orders to proceed farther east.

A report came in that in the Greek port of Navarino three large transports were making ready for sea—so off went *Sokol* to investigate matters.

The port was well guarded and, as further protection, a gigantic wire net had been sunk over the harbor entrance below the surface. Behind this net lay the three big transports, and with them two large destroyers of the *Alvieri* class.

Commander Karnicki decided that the prizes offered were too good to miss. Submerging his boat, he crept carefully into the harbor after dark, only to find himself caught in the antisubmarine net. Overhead, he could hear the scream of propellers as motor torpedo boats hunted for *Sokol* tangled in the meshes; soon depth charges began to explode. The thuds were some distance from the boat, and the commander judged it fair to assume that his actual whereabouts were unknown.

All the time he was maneuvering the ship, and finally, with superb skill, he freed her and rose nearer to one of the destroyers which was now prepared to take part in the hunt.

There came a blinding explosion. Two torpedoes from the *Sokol* had struck the destroyer, a big vessel of 1,900 tons. The two simultaneous hits were too much for her, and she disappeared in a cloud of smoke and flame, while the *Sokol* dived deep, to lie snug while surface craft scurried about, dropping their depth charges in the wildest confusion all over the harbor, and guns ashore began to fire at an unknown target.

Commander Karnicki was not the man to lose an opportunity of this kind. While the Italians were in a state of complete panic, he maneuvered his submarine to another part of the harbor and coolly fired more torpedoes at the second destroyer and also at one of the transports.

Through the periscope he watched his torpedoes strike home. The big transport was struck fairly amidships and burst into flames. Soldiers and sailors, panic-stricken, jumped from her decks into the sea and began to swim for the shore as the vessel, a liner of between 5,000 and 6,000 tons, heeled over and sank.

The second destroyer had also been hit amidships and was blazing fiercely. It is considered highly probable that she, too, went down, but Commander Karnicki does not claim her as a definite sinking. All he does claim is that she was badly damaged and probably sank. He could not remain inside the harbor long enough to report exactly what happened to her.

He was compelled to make his way out to the open sea while the panic and confusion lasted.

Barring his way once more was the big wire net, which he would have either to pass over or to force a way through.

Firing from the shore guns was coming in all directions as he took his submarine clear of the inner harbor and began the nerve-racking business of negotiating the net. But the shells from the Italian guns did not cause him much real uneasiness, for most of them were crashing into the sea in exactly the opposite direction from that in which the *Sokol* was maneuvering. It was obvious that the Italians had not located her and were firing blindly in the hope that a lucky shot might land on the target. Later, it was believed, with good reason, that in their excitement the gunners were chiefly aiming at one of their own small MTB's, which they mistook in the darkness for an enemy craft.

Unscathed, the *Sokol* got clear of the harbor and the net, and lay submerged at the bottom. There her commander decided to await developments. And he did not wait long.

The day passed quietly, but when darkness fell the next night, the remaining transport was heard coming from the harbor. She was escorted by MTB's, a sure sign that even if the second destroyer had not actually been sunk, she had been far too badly damaged to put to sea as an escort. Conditions for attack were far more favorable, but Commander Karnicki was not the type of man to allow a full laden transport to pass unmolested. He watched her closely—a ship of about 4,000 tons, around whom the MTB's were circling like sheep dogs guarding a flock.

The *Sokol* waited until the transport was directly abreast of her as she lay submerged at periscope depth, and then several torpedoes were let loose.

They were dead on the target, and the transport began to sink rapidly immediately after the first explosion. Again panic broke out as men jumped from the sinking ship, and the shore batteries broke out again, firing wildly. But the *Sokol* had vanished once more beneath the water, leaving the Italians bewildered.

Not content with this, she proceeded during that same night to attack two more transports and, if they were not sunk, they were certainly damaged.

After that, *Sokol* resumed her cruise. The routes which the Italian vessels followed were pretty well known to the British and Allied submarines operating in the Mediterranean, thanks to the constant air patrols, and soon the *Sokol* found herself in a well-used "lane."

Before long she saw an Italian auxiliary cruiser, of about 4,000 tons, obviously making at high speed for an Italian base. For her the *Sokol* lay in wait, and sent three torpedoes into her hull. In full view of the Poles on board the submarine, another 5,000 tons of enemy shipping went to the bottom of the Mediterranean.

The next victim was a 3,500-ton supply ship loaded with arms and munitions for Rommel's *Afrika Korps*. The supply ship was trying to make the run under cover of darkness without an escort, relying on her speed to outwit attack. But the Polish submarine intercepted her on the surface and fired her gun, sending shells crashing through the steamer's hull and onto her deck. The Italian stopped and her crew abandoned her. There was no need to waste torpedoes on such a ship. Commander Karnicki decided instead to board her, take her papers, and then sink her with an explosive charge.

When he investigated, he found her to be carrying high explosives —several thousand tons of shells were packed in her holds. That little lot never reached Rommel. There was a blinding flash, a deafening roar—and the end of the supply ship.

Not unnaturally, as the result of these spectacular sinkings, *Sokol* became one of the most hunted submarines in the Mediterranean. Both the Italians and the Germans considered her commander to be far too resourceful and daring a man to be allowed to cruise freely.

But such was his good fortune that he was soon known as "Lucky Bob" and the ship as *Lucky Sokol*.

She had scores of narrow escapes from destruction, but what was possibly her closest shave from disaster came when she was based on Malta during the worst period of the air attacks.

Sokol had just returned from a patrol off the island of Lampedusa and was moored in the harbor when enemy planes came over on a grand scale. There were daily attacks on Malta. Several big bombs fell within a few feet of the submarine, but did no serious damage.

But *Sokol* had to be taken into the yards for repairs, the work occupying fourteen days and nights, and during that time the invaders were continuously over the island, raining down high explosives. Despite the constant crash of bombs, both the shipyard workmen and the *Sokol's* own crew continued operations and finally had her ready for sea again.

She left the shipyard and was undergoing the process of demagnetization when a number of Ju-88's came in to attack.

The *Sokol* was exposed to view, and as soon as they spotted her the planes dived to deliver low-level attacks. Bombs of heavy caliber crashed all around the ship, causing serious damage and injuring a number of the officers and crew. Water flooded the accumulators, and soon the interior of the submarine was filled with poisonous gas, while boiling sulfuric acid streamed from the batteries. The whole ship was plunged into darkness by the breaking of the electrical installation and plant.

Soon a still more dangerous situation developed. The heat was intense and increasing. Hydrogen was accumulating in the damaged batteries and was likely to cause an explosion at any moment and set the submarine ablaze.

She had already got her full complement of torpedoes and shells on board, and these were in grave danger of exploding, due to the action of the heat and the constant vibration caused by the bombs. The crew were forced to wear their gas masks to protect them from the poisonous atmosphere, laden with a combination of smoke and chlorine gas.

No help was available from the shore and it seemed as if the ship were doomed. But not a man suggested leaving her.

"We've got to save her," declared the commander.

Their only hope was to get fresh air pumped into the hull to expel the poisonous fumes, clear the hull of the acid and salt water which constituted the real danger, and then unload the torpedoes and other explosives.

One of the engineers reported that the diesel engines were undamaged and could quickly be got working. He suggested that they should attempt what had hitherto been considered an impossible feat.

"Get the engines working," he said, "connect the electrical generators with the main electrical network and ventilate the batteries, and while this is being done pump the acid and water from the ship and disconnect the damaged batteries."

Experts had never considered it feasible to connect the generators directly with the complete electrical network. It was thought that the generators must be connected only with the batteries, owing to the grave risk of burning out not only the generators themselves but the whole complicated electrical system.

"It's a risk worth taking," commented Commander Karnicki. "Who'll volunteer for the job?"

Every man of the crew volunteered. But only two officers and five petty officers and ratings were chosen. For two hours, in intense heat and wearing gas masks, they toiled. At any moment the ship might have blown up, but not a man left his job. Then the engines were started up and for a few moments of suspense the crew stood by and waited to learn the result of their experiment. Would the current generated be too strong and result in the destruction of all the machinery on board and possibly the ship herself?

The engines were nursed carefully to control the generation of the current. The fans were switched on, the pumps started to work. Salt water and acid began to pour over the side, fresh air supplanted the poisonous fumes that filled the ship, while bombs fell all the time.

It was a desperate, dangerous contest, but courage and determination won. The *Sokol* returned to the repair yard for overhaul.

But the worst was not over. Day and night the enemy intensified his efforts to reduce Malta. Soon the shipyard in which the *Sokol* was being refitted was marked out as a special target for the bomb-aimers. The workers, many of whom fell victim to the heavy rain of high explosive, were obliged to seek shelter during the worst periods of the raids, but not so the officers and men of the *Sokol*. They refused to take cover, but worked on, unloading the ruined batteries, fitting new ones, replacing all damaged equipment, and repairing leaks caused by concussion.

One member of the crew was killed and several others were wounded by bomb splinters, but still the work went on.

Constantly the vessel was subjected to low-level attack and dive-bombing. It became necessary to remove her from the repair yard to a hiding place some distance away, where under a camouflage of nets and canvas she might remain unseen. But her anchorage had to be changed daily.

Once, when she was lying hidden among a number of barges in harbor, bombs fell within a few feet, tearing away the nets and canvas camouflage and sinking several of the barges. Again serious damage was caused. Her hull had deep dents and holes torn in it, and her electric cables were made useless.

Work had to be resumed on these, and it continued day and night in spite of the bombings. Only the boundless courage and devotion of the officers and crew of that vessel brought her through the ordeal. Time and again they had to stand by and see the result of hours of ceaseless toil in intense heat and danger destroyed in a few seconds. They cursed, but never despaired.

In their efforts to get their ship fit for sea again, they were helped by officers and men of the Royal Navy, who volunteered to help in the repairs when they were free of their regular duties.

At last came a day when, although she was in no fit condition to proceed to sea, *Sokol* could at least dive to the bottom of the harbor and so perhaps escape the attention of the dive bombers, who were more than ever determined on her destruction.

In deep water she lay hidden while bombers roared overhead. When they disappeared she surfaced, and further repair work was carried out.

At that time it was not possible to complete fully the necessary work that would render her fit to resume operations while she remained in Malta. The nearest base where the job could be completed was a thousand miles away, but, nevertheless, unseaworthy though she was, and in no fit condition to offer even an efficient defense if she were attacked, Commander Karnicki decided to make an attempt at the voyage.

He knew the dangers of minefields and the even greater dangers of aerial attack, for at that time German and Italian planes were continually patrolling the Mediterranean, and there was a specially tough spot off the Sicilian coast, where an extensive minefield had been laid.

When the *Sokol* sailed from Malta she had a single battery of the entire electrical equipment in working order, and only one propeller could operate. This meant that she could only travel submerged a little more than 20 miles in twelve hours, and at a rather faster rate when surfaced.

Off the real danger zone, the Sicilian coast, Commander Karnicki resolved on taking the boldest possible course in order to get away from the area as quickly as possible. Instead of diving deeply to avoid the minefield, he made the whole run at nighttime on the surface at a distance of between 3 and 5 miles from the coast. He explained later on that he had decided to take this risk rather than face the possibility of sustaining serious and irreparable damage by taking the craft deeper than 60 feet down, which was in his opinion the utmost depth to which she could go in the condition she was in. And a depth of 60 feet in a minefield was useless.

"She could not have withstood the pressure on her hull at any great depth," he said. "In fact, I was astonished that she stood up to any pressure at all."

Naturally the crew were well aware of the dangers which they faced on that trip, but not a man displayed the slightest anxiety as to the outcome.

"We were sailing with 'Lucky Bob' in the *Lucky Sokol*," they commented.

Before leaving Malta they laid in a big stock of nuts. Members of submarine crews cannot smoke owing to the necessity for keeping the air as free from contamination as possible. But they can and do eat nuts and sweets. The normal monthly ration of the English civilian would disappear in a few minutes if given to a man on board a submarine.

Those nuts on board the *Sokol* got on Commander Karnicki's nerves. He could not tolerate the constant cracking of their shells. As is so well known, it is the little things which count in the reaction that follows serious strain.

"Bob" put an end to the nuisance by issuing an order prohibiting the eating of nuts, and until the *Sokol* reached her new base the crew had to be content with a small daily issue of sweets.

And when she did reach her base, the experts voiced their astonishment as they completed their examination, for she had come through unscathed.

"She is not fit to proceed a single mile at sea," they pronounced, "much less dive, even to periscope depth. The wonder is that she ever got through!"

But the *Sokol* went back into commission, and her gallant crew continued to defy the efforts of the Germans to destroy them and their ship.

She was the first Allied ship to enter Brindisi and send ashore her British liaison officer with two Polish ratings. The Italian admiral in command of the port was very surprised to see a vessel flying an "unknown" ensign. Afterward he did all he could to satisfy their demands. The *Sokol* sent another boarding party to an Italian submarine and directed her to Malta. Another submarine and several transport vessels followed and safely made British ports under *Sokol's* escort.

In October, 1943, *Sokol* sank two German ships, totaling 11,000 tons, in the Adriatic.

The high opinions which the British and the Polish Admiralty here hold of the commander and crew is shown by the fact that no fewer than nine British and thirty-seven Polish decorations have been awarded to different members of the ship's company—a rare distinction, even in the submarine service.

When the Germans overran Holland in World War II, all the Dutch submarines in Europe that were able to joined the British submarine service. Those in the Dutch East Indies joined either the British or U.S. submarine force in Australia. Without exception the Dutch crews proved their mettle. That they also proved their humanity and humor is shown in this story of their treatment of some German submarine prisoners of war.

O-21 Evens the Score

RICHARD BAXTER

IN submarine operations luck counts for a good deal.

The captain of the Dutch submarine *O-21* was merely following his luck when he fell in with the German U-boat *U-95* in the extreme western Mediterranean.

The *U-95* was a new German submarine which had been first commissioned at Kiel during August, 1940. Her commander, *Kapitaenleutnant* Gert Schreiber, holder of the Iron Cross, First Class, was one of Germany's ace submarine commanders and a close friend of Prien, the submarine captain who claimed the distinction of being the Pride of the German Navy, since he claimed the record for sinkings of Allied vessels.

Prien, it will be remembered, was lost in the Atlantic in 1940 during a brief encounter with a British destroyer.

Schreiber had taken the *U-95*, a vessel of 500 tons with a complement of forty-five officers and men, including two midshipmen who were training to become submarine officers, on November 16, 1941. Eight days later he was crawling through the Strait of Gibraltar, her periscope down, the submarine sailing blind in order to escape the vigilance of the British lookout. Safely through the Narrows, the *U-95* headed east and looked around for something to sink.

Schreiber was anxious to add to the total of 60,000 tons of merchant shipping which he claimed to have sunk since he had commanded the *U-95*, and he was convinced that he would find numerous victims if he lay in wait just east of Gibraltar.

On a brilliant moonlit night, with the sea like glass, *U-95* surfaced in order to recharge her batteries and blow fresh air into the vessel.

Schreiber and twelve of the crew were on deck or on the bridge, enjoying the moonlight on November 28, when the lookout on board the Dutch craft spotted them. The *O-21* had surfaced and was moving slowly eastward, making for the track usually followed by enemy shipping. When the *U-95* was first seen, she was rather more than three miles distant from the *O-21* and it was not possible to identify her definitely as an enemy.

But the commander of the Dutch craft was not taking any chances. Carefully fixing the position of the unknown submarine, he ordered the *O-21* to dive to below periscope depth, and very cautiously moved his vessel in the direction of the mystery ship before raising his periscope again to have a fresh look. He knew that if the slightest sound were heard by those on board the stranger, she would crash-dive at once and all hope of attacking her successfully would have to be abandoned.

By skillful navigation, though his progress was necessarily blind, the Dutch captain brought his submarine to within a few hundred yards of the German, and then raising his periscope he was able to identify her without doubt as an enemy.

His crew were already at action stations and the torpedo tubes were ready for firing.

The crew of the *U-95* had not heard the Dutch vessel approach. They were lounging on the deck in the bright moonlight, and the commander stood leaning over the rail of the little bridge. She was lying broadside on to the *O-21*, a splendid "sitting" target.

"Fire!" came the order, and instantly two torpedoes were winging their way rapidly through the glassy water.

The first torpedo scraped by the side of the *U-95* but did not explode. The second, however, hit her full on the stern. There was a blinding flash, a deafening explosion, and the stern of *U-95* was torn away and sank. Six seconds later the rest of the German followed; her bows were elevated high in the air and she slid gently on end below the surface, while huge bubbles of air followed by great patches of black oil appeared in due course.

One man in the German submarine was actually in the conning tower, about to go on deck when the torpedo struck home. He was literally blown out of the conning tower and into the water. Schreiber and those of his officers and men who were actually on deck were thrown into the sea by the force of the explosion, and all started to swim to the *O-21*, which had now surfaced. Each of the men was wearing a life jacket, and they were all hauled on board, prisoners and half stupefied.

Once on the deck of the Dutch submarine, Schreiber, a typical twenty-nine-year-old German, became arrogant and boastful. He gave a contemptuous look at the captain of the Dutch vessel which had sunk his own and then turned his back on him.

"Search the prisoners," ordered the Dutch captain.

One of the Dutch petty officers ordered the Germans to stand in a row on the narrow deck, whereupon Schreiber intervened and gave an order in German, which was not understood by the Dutch seamen. The prisoners promptly grouped themselves round their captain, who began to harangue them.

The Dutch captain was in no mood to allow anyone but himself to give orders to his prisoners.

"I do not allow speeches on board my ship," he promptly informed Schreiber, who observed with a sneer:

"I will pass on any orders which you may give to my own crew."

"I repeat," said the Dutchman calmly, "that in this ship I give the orders. Let that be clearly understood."

Without further ado, the twelve prisoners of war were bundled below deck under armed guard and there carefully searched.

In order to carry out the searching, it was necessary for the prisoners to remove their lifesaving jackets. Against this they protested vigorously.

"It is not safe," they argued. "We shall need them."

"You won't." The Dutch seamen laughed. "Nor shall we."

"They must be given back to us," stipulated one of the German officers. "They will be absolutely necessary when we go to Canada, where the British are sending all their prisoners. No ships with prisoners can get to Canada owing to our blockade, and if we are not allowed our jackets, we shall drown."

"Wouldn't that be a pity?" remarked one stalwart Dutch seaman.

"Ever think of the innocent civilians who have drowned through such as you?"

"You need have no fear of drowning," put in the Dutch captain. "The British ships are getting through safely despite your submarines. You will be well looked after."

There was an even funnier side to this rescue.

In the little wardroom of the *O-21* was a large photograph of Mr. Winston Churchill, one of the treasured possessions of the officers and crew.

Schreiber was seated at the table directly facing this photograph. Before him had been set a meal and a steaming mug of coffee. He was just raising this to his lips when he noticed the photograph for the first time. Instantly he put down the mug, stared hard at the picture, and then said:

"Take that thing away. The eyes follow me everywhere."

"Don't you like looking at the British Prime Minister?" they asked him.

"I will not look at him," he declared, almost hysterically. "Take it down instantly."

"The picture stays," they told him.

"Then I shall not eat till it has been removed," he replied. "And nor will any of my crew."

"Splendid." The Dutchman laughed. "That may enable us to stay at sea a little longer and perhaps allow us to sink more ships. Food is rather a problem in a submarine—don't you think so, Herr *Kapitaenleutnant*?"

"Take the picture down!" he ordered—but it remained where it was.

So, much to the amusement of the Dutch, the Germans solemnly went on hunger strike.

That hunger strike lasted four days, after which, although the picture of the Prime Minister still hung in the wardroom, they were glad enough to eat.

For sinking the *U-95*, the Dutch captain, who already held the D.S.O., was awarded the bar, his lieutenant was given the D.S.C., and a torpedo artificer and a seaman each got the D.S.M.

Although the Dutch captain does not claim to have sunk anything like the amount of tonnage claimed by his prisoner, it is officially admitted that his score is upwards of 30,000 tons.

Few submarine crews have had to endure the twin hell of a shattered ship and inhuman treatment in a prisoner-of-war camp. Grenadier's crew and her courageous captain endured the worst their captors could dish out. Only a handful survived, but all remained men to the last.

She Was a Grand Ship

EDITORS OF *NAVY TIMES*

"Submarine attacks," wrote Fleet Admiral Ernest J. King, Chief of the United States Fleet and Chief of Naval Operations, "produced immediate and damaging results . . . made it more difficult for the enemy to consolidate his forward positions, to reinforce his threatened areas, and to pile up in Japan an adequate reserve of fuel oil, rubber, and other loot from his newly conquered territory."

By the end of 1944, Japan's merchant fleet was less than half of what she required to wage war. The number of United States submarines, meanwhile, had increased nearly 40 per cent over the 1941 total although as our forces captured more territory, the Pacific hunting preserve grew smaller and smaller.

High priority was accorded the destruction of Japanese destroyers, with the result that more destroyers were sunk by submarines than by any other means. The underwater boats also performed notable work in rescuing downed airmen. More than 500 Allied aviators were plucked from the sea during the war.

The cost of victory, however, remained dear. And of all the sacrifices made by our fighting forces, that of being taken prisoner was the most exacting. It did not happen often to submarine crews, but one of the exceptions involved the *Grenadier*.

Her thirty-five-year-old skipper was a former intercollegiate boxing champion, Lt. Comdr. John A. Fitzgerald, small of stature but a determined scrapper. Behind the *Grenadier* lay five war patrols and 42,710 tons of sunken enemy shipping—ten ships plus one plane—

when she nosed into Lem Valon Strait off the west coast of the Malay Peninsula the night of April 21, 1943. At about 9 P.M. the officer of the deck saw smoke. The *Grenadier* continued on her westerly course until two enemy merchantmen were sighted.

Fitzgerald tracked the ships and, guessing their maneuvering tactics, moved the *Grenadier* on the surface to a spot which would put her in an attack position at the right time.

But fifteen minutes before the submarine was to dive and attack, a lookout cried, "Plane, port quarter." Fitzgerald ordered the *Grenadier* down.

The submarine was descending; it had passed 120 feet. Fitzgerald recalls that just as Lt. George H. Whiting, the executive officer, was saying, "We ought to be safe now," it seemed as though two express trains collided. A 500-kilogram depth charge had detonated nearby.

"The force of the explosion heeled the boat over 10 to 15 degrees," the skipper continued. "All lights and power were lost. I continued on down. At about 200 feet the word was received, 'fire in maneuvering room.' I set the boat down on the bottom at 267 feet of water."

Fitzgerald was thankful for the shallows in this part of the Pacific. The fire was stubborn, however, resisting first attempts to extinguish it. For half an hour, the maneuvering room was sealed off, then reopened to allow a bucket brigade inside, eventually bringing the flames and smoke under control. However, a damaged valve allowed a stream of water to pour into the control stand, and spray over the electrical equipment. A bucket brigade was set up between the maneuvering room and the forward torpedo room to keep the water level down below the motors.

The strenuous work in the oven-like atmosphere soon took its toll. One man after another fell unconscious, and others stepped into their places in the feverish efforts to save the motors. Finally a rig was set up between the main battery and a drain pump to keep down the water level below that of the main motors. The exhausted bucket brigade was able to stop its labor and tend to those who had collapsed.

The maneuvering-room after bulkhead had taken the force of the explosion and had been badly damaged, as was the after torpedo room loading hatch, which let a shower of water into the torpedo room. All the after tubes were knocked out of commission; all hy-

97

draulic lines to the tubes, vents, and steering mechanism were ruptured.

This damage was equaled throughout the boat. The radio-room equipment was shattered and the crew's messroom was a shambles of broken dishes and phonograph records.

Smoke filled the submarine.

About 9:30 P.M., after the *Grenadier* had been under almost thirteen hours, Fitzgerald surfaced his craft and tried to clear the boat by using the main engines to create suction. Work on the damaged submarine continued throughout the night, but about 5 A.M. the engineer and the electricians reported to Fitzgerald on the bridge that their efforts to regain propulsion had been fruitless. The electric cables had been ruined through fire and salt water.

Fitzgerald considered trying to set up a sail to let the breeze carry the *Grenadier* closer to the beach where he could disembark the crew and blow up the boat. However, this effort was abandoned as it seemed to be futile.

As the *Grenadier* sat on the surface, a ship approached from the northwest out of Lem Valon Strait. It seemed to be a large destroyer or light cruiser. Then smoke from a patrol ship or an escort vessel was seen in the southeast.

Fitzgerald had to decide whether to take his submarine back down without power, or to abandon.

Before either operation could be started, a light bomber zoomed out of the sky to strafe the *Grenadier*. But this sitting duck struck back with two 20-mm. and two .30-caliber machine guns. Though hit three times, the plane pulled its nose up sharply and positioned for a run on the stricken boat's port side. The submariners continued their fire, but the aircraft came in directly overhead and unloaded its bombs before heading off in the direction of Penang, where it crashed.

The nearest bomb exploded in the water less than 100 yards from the submarine.

Fitzgerald ordered all hands to line up forward of the conning tower, leaving the chief of the boat, William Clyde Withrow, below to flood the safety tank. When the ship from the northwest, which turned out to be an 1,800-ton Japanese merchantman, was within about two miles of the *Grenadier*, Fitzgerald ordered the officers and crew over the side. Withrow opened the main vents and escaped before the submarine went down, stern first. Fitzgerald, in the best tradition of the sea, was the last over. Since there was only one small rubber raft available, the men used their Momsen escape lungs as life preservers.

A large subchaser joined the enemy merchantman and the patrol vessel. The ships steamed toward the submarine's 68 men and 8 officers while Lt. Kevin D. Harty "clung to a mattress, reading the *Readers' Digest* to us," according to Chief Yeoman Robert W. Palmer of San Francisco.

The ships circled and photographed the submariners before the enemy merchantman picked them up via a jacob's ladder, stripped them, and searched their belongings. Buoys were dropped over the spot where the *Grenadier* vanished under the waves.

The merchantman then continued on its way to Penang, Malaya, and arrived there the morning of April 24 with its hungry, tired, and discouraged prisoners.

"We were spared because they wanted information from us." Palmer reported, "We were marched onto the dock and taken to what once was a British school. In about a half hour a Nip officer showed up with a club and brandished it. We were stood in a zigzag row and clubbed for the slightest movement of the body or eyelash until late evening. Then our positions were changed to hands over head, knees bent. We had had no food since our capture.

"Then the clubbing became more frequent. The men were taken one at a time to a room, the door of which was marked 'Art Room,' and tortured by clubbing with the flat of a sword and a round club. Matches were stuck under fingernails. We were tied across a three-quarter bed, face down, and worked over with clubs. They would lash a man to a bench tilted at a 20-degree angle, head down, and pour water down his nose. Fitzgerald really went through hell for us. They beat him, jumped on his stomach, and stuck knife blades under his nails. He never talked, except to cuss out the Jap commander; and they put him to work unloading coal from their ships and cracking rocks for that.

"This treatment continued for five days and nights without food. On the evening of the fifth night, we got wormy rice broth. No smokes. Occasionally, a 'good' guard would let us lie down for an hour, then awaken us with the butt of his gun.

"They asked the skipper for the location of other subs, for call signals and frequencies. Some of the men did give erroneous information, such as the name of the submarine as the 'Goldfish.'"

The officers and enlisted men were kept apart but they used the same toilet. Whenever the captain went there he scribbled messages to the crew on the bulkhead, such as "Don't tell 'em anything," "Keep your heads up," and "Guard the T.D.C." The T.D.C. was the Target Data Computer, one of the Navy's secret mechanisms which was used to establish and hit the target.

"We ate hedge blossoms, stems, and grass," Palmer continued. "We ate Listerine toothpaste mixed with tobacco for Mother's Day.

"After the eighth day, the treatment changed from purposeful questioning to individual sadistic satisfaction of the Nip guards, like sitting on deck, hands on knees, and staring rigidly ahead. Also, all men were put into a circle with head between the legs of the man next to him, and then made to crawl about the cement deck imitating a train and animals until our knees and hands were raw.

"We had no baths; we still got rice broth at 8 A.M. and 9 P.M. This treatment continued for two months. Men became weak and they were beaten. Then two or four weak men were put on a table and the rest had to hold it over their heads. The guards were Formosa Nips. They wanted our jewelry and made us wish we had given it to them. We were in Penang, and under this treatment for four months."

On July 18, 1943, the survivors left Penang for Singapore in a filthy ship, arriving three days later. They worked at the Singapore Naval Base until September 26, when they were put aboard another filthy ship, *Asama Maru*, and taken on a seventeen-day voyage to Japan.

"Two days out of Japan they tortured the men beyond all comprehension," said Palmer. "We arrived at Shimoda Saki on October 10 and divided. Twenty-nine men were sent to Ofuna Interrogation Camp, where they encountered Fitzgerald, Whiting, and Harty, who had previously been flown there. The remaining men remained in a steel mill at Shimoda Saki.

"Ofuna was another nine months of hell. High-ranking officers were at this camp, but no distinction was made as to care and treatment. They and we were put to work in the Ashio copper mines. The treatment continued as usual—death and torture.

"There was no medicine. Working hours were from 5 A.M. to

8 P.M. We got two days a month off. All the men who died were cremated. Food conditions during the last six months of the war were acute . . . the Jap civilians were starving, too. Our morale, by this time, was rock bottom and our thoughts and dreams were of food."

In a group statement, for Navy records, seventeen other *Grenadier* crew members noted: "By the end of June we were all swollen up with beriberi . . . One guard whom we called 'Banana Nose' was truly a sadist. 'Banana Nose' had a pal whom we called 'Gold Tooth,' and it was from these two monsters that we received our most insensate treatment . . . We started working in the steel mills. . . . Four of our crew died there, mostly from malnutrition. They seemed to have a personal grudge against the submarine men, because when anything went wrong they would take it out on us. We figured they had a good reason for this due to the success of our submarines blockading their shipping. There is one man, Dr. Herbert A. Markowitz (lieutenant, junior grade), who will always live in our minds. He worked night and day taking care of us. Sometimes it was even necessary for him to steal medical supplies to care for the sick."

Warren E. Roberts, a torpedoman, second class, remembered: "When we got to Nagasaki we were placed in a Japanese navy camp. The treatment was pretty rough here. They ran us up and down the highway with no shoes on in front of people who threw stones at us. No one ever received any of the Red Cross supplies because the Japs sold everything. We were first bombed in August of 1944 (at Yawata). We had no air raid shelters. We were put up in a second story of a pipe shop. Shrapnel was constantly beating down on this shop. Then they let us go down and get into a hole. They consistently told us that, because we were submarine men, they were getting their revenge on us."

And so their torment continued—torture and privation—which was to claim but four of the *Grenadier's* original complement.

No book of submarine exploits would be complete without a story about Lt. Comdr. M. E. Nasmith. During World War I he was one of the world's most experienced submarine officers. Nasmith was also one of the most popular officers in the British submarine service. He did things with a submarine that seem virtually impossible. His exploits in the E-11 in the Sea of Marmara nearly drove Turkish ships out of this, their own private sea. This story begins after Nasmith had successfully penetrated the minefields in the Straits of Dardanelles and had begun his patrol in the Sea of Marmara.

Singeing the Sultan's Beard

W. G. CARR

REMEMBERING the annoyance caused *E-14* by Turkish patrol boats, Nasmith captured a small sailing vessel soon after getting safely through the straits. Trimming the submarine down till only her conning tower was awash, he made his captive fast alongside. *E-11* was now, from the east, simply an innocent dhow which proceeded mysteriously on her way whatever the wind or lack of it. Behind this screen a hopeful lookout was kept for anything that floated, but the ruse was unsuccessful. Knowing of the crashing of the Narrows by another submarine, the Turk kept to his harbors. After a day of masquerade the dhow was turned back to her relieved crew, and Nasmith returned to the westward.

For two days nothing happened. Neither color of sail nor smudge of smoke was sighted. It seemed as if *E-14*'s conquests had cleaned the sea of traffic. On the twenty-third, however, the dull days ended. Early in the morning *E-11* was off Oxia Island, a few miles south of the entrance to the Bosporus. A small dhow was sighted, and while busy with her an empty transport was sighted to the north, making for Constantinople. Forsaking the smaller prey for the larger, Nasmith gave chase.

The next hour was a thrilling one. The dhow had been sighted around 3:30 A.M., the transport sighted a little after four. Eight miles

102

away lay Constantinople still hidden by the quickly loosening night. The water was deadly calm. The periscope dare split the sea for seconds only. Ahead was the ungainly transport; to the east, clarion color waiting for the sun. At some one moment when he ordered "Raise periscope" Nasmith, his eye glued to the rubber eyepiece, must have seen the first level rays of sunrise crown the mosques and minarets with gold.

Around six the transport was abandoned for better quarry. A Turkish gunboat, *Pelenk-i-Dria,* was observed off Constantinople. *E-11* maneuvered for a shot, and loosed the port-bow torpedo. It was a clean hit, and the Turkish sailors, gamely manning a six-pounder gun, opened fire on the contemptuously raised periscope. It was here that the damage occurred. The first round hit the foremost periscope. An extraordinary shot. Proceeding to *E-14's* preening ground off Kalolimni, the damage was repaired and the crew allowed a much-needed bath.

Communications were reestablished with the *Jed* on the twenty-fourth. Captain Nasmith's most cherished story of his entire trip in the Sea of Marmara had to do with an encounter on this day. Late in the morning a small steamer was sighted and ordered to stop. She ignored the order. *E-11,* having no gun mounted, was forced to come to the surface and rely on the dependable rifle. The effect of a few rounds of small-arms fire was startling. The crew took to the boats in a panic. Two were capsized getting them into the water.

The crew of *E-11* cursed the men for their clumsiness, and lent a hand to help them right their boats. During the confusion a sedate, calm figure appeared on the upper deck. With a scrupulous regard for social etiquette he made no attempt to speak until spoken to. Neither did he show the least concern at being the one remaining person on board. He was certainly no Turk.

When asked for explanations, he introduced himself, "Silas Q. Swing of the Chicago *Sun,*" and tendered his card over the ship's side to prove it. He then objected to the inconvenience *E-11* was causing him. Duty and a waiting world required that he get to Chanak and find out what was happening there. Asked if the steamer had any supplies on board, he sensibly replied that he had no idea what was on board. Nor did he give a damn, it appeared.

Mr. Swing impressed Nasmith very much. Nasmith always said that Swing must have been the world's most unobservant journalist.

"When D'Oyly Hughes, my first lieutenant, went on board, the first thing he saw was a six-inch gun lashed across one of the hatchways. The mounting was located in the forehold, and in the after hold was a plentiful supply of ammunition to fit it. On deck were cases marked 'Krupp.'" Mr. Swing was invited to join the crew in the righted boats and forget about Chanak. The waiting world would have to wait. Hughes placed a demolition charge, and Swing saw his means of transportation slide out of sight.

Before the swelling eddy of her going had smoothed away, they sighted the smoke of another steamer, gave chase, and found her a storeship heading for Rodosto, the largest Turkish port on the north shore of the Marmara. She evidently thought if she could make the harbor she would be safe. But she wasn't. *E-11* came to the surface and chased her till she was tied up alongside her pier. With a gun it would have been a simple matter to finish her, but the submarine had no gun. Nasmith submerged and discovered there was none too much water to swim about in. She was hitting the bottom rather heavily, and he was forced to expose the periscope more than was healthy with the fire coming from the shore.

However, the ship was an important prize. Her decks were laden high with packing cases destined for troops on the peninsula. Luck was with Nasmith again. One successful shot and she broke into flames. The submarine, with her conning tower exposed at times because of the shallowness of the water, proceeded out of the bay.

Within ten minutes a third steamer was sighted. When ordered to stop she attempted to ram and, failing, ran for the shore, where she grounded. Here *E-11* had her first taste of the amphibian warfare she was later to become adept in. A demolition party was preparing to board the beached steamer when a party of Turkish cavalry appeared on the cliffs. Bullets rained down from above and Nasmith felt for once that discretion was the better part of valor.

Thanks to Silas Q. Swing, the rumor was already abroad in Constantinople that eleven British submarines were operating in the Sea of Marmara when *E-11* herself arrived in the harbor. She was the first enemy of any description to intrude on the sacred precincts of the Golden Horn in the five hundred years the Turks had held the city. Nasmith's own account is a classic of maddening brevity. "So," he wrote, "we dived unobserved into Constantinople." The word "so" refers to the disgust the crew of *E-11* felt when they could find nothing but small fry out in the open.

Nasmith raised periscope shortly after noon in the center of the harbor, and immediately there occurred one of those incongruous incidents which pleased him. "Our maneuvering," he used to say, was rather difficult because of the cross tides, the mud, and the current, but most particularly on account of a damn fool of a fisherman who kept trying to grab the top of my periscope every time I raised it to take an observation. I don't think he had any idea what it was, but to get rid of him I gave him a chance to get a good hold on it. Then I ordered 'Down periscope quickly' and almost succeeded in capsizing his boat. When I looked at him a minute later he wore the most amazed and bewildered expression I ever hope to see."

The Arabian Nights entertainment did not end with the adventure of *E-11* and the modern Sinbad the Sailor. Rising close to the United States ship *Scorpion*, a good-sized vessel was seen close to the arsenal. Nasmith fired the port-bow tube. The torpedo developed a gyro failure, which means that the gear which governed her direction failed, locking the rudder hard over.

Nasmith said that the torpedo went chasing around the harbor, acting like nothing so much as a hen with its head cut off. Round and round it went at a speed of 47 knots, and every few seconds it switched from hen to porpoise and jumped out of the water. "It was bound to hit something, and by the look of things it was just as likely to be us as anything else."

So he fired the starboard-bow tube. By this time the harbor was in an uproar, and if ever a submarine was in a delicate position it was *E-11* at that moment. But Nasmith did a thing which I never heard equaled for sheer nerve. The moment he fired the torpedo at the ship loading by the arsenal wharf, he put a small camera to the eyepiece of the periscope and took a picture of the munition ship blowing up. The first torpedo hit something and exploded at the same time.

"The enemy was given to issuing false reports about any successes we claimed," I have heard him explain. "They were experts at propaganda and counterpropaganda. So we could reap the full moral effect of going into their precious harbor and blowing their ships to Hades as they laid moored safely inside, we tried taking some exposures with the camera lens close to the eyepiece of the periscope."

I saw the photograph. You could see the munition ship enveloped in a cloud of smoke with debris flying as high as the masthead. The sensitive film had also registered the cross wires and degree marks on the periscope lens which are used for judging distances and for taking bearings.

There was little question of the moral effect of *E-11*'s astonishing exploit. Although the *Stambul* which she had sunk was an old ship, and was possibly beached before she sank, the city was thrown into a state of panic, troops were ordered off transports, and all sea traffic between Constantinople and the peninsula was virtually stopped.

Getting out of Constantinople was infinitely more exciting than getting in there. Once certain of his kill, Nasmith gave the order to dive. Down she sank and then grounded heavily.

"Then we bounced 30 feet, if the depth indicators were to be believed," to recall Nasmith's own story again. "I went down and sat on the bottom. Then a strange thing happened. We looked at the compass to discover our best course, and we noticed we were altering course rapidly even though we were right on the bottom. We were swinging right around the compass card. We watched this happening with great interest. It was evident that we must be resting on the shoal under Leander Tower, judging by the depth, and were being turned by the current unless something had succeeded in hooking on to us and was towing us. This was a disquieting thought, so we started the motors and bumped our way gently off the shoal, sank into about 85 feet of water, and proceeded as requisite out of the harbor."

And when they were safely out of the harbor and out of the narrow waters of the Golden Horn they headed for the quieter reaches in the center of the Sea of Marmara by Kalolimni. Here they rested the next day, charged their batteries, and washed and bathed. Nasmith told me, and I know from experience, what a godsend it was to bathe and change into clean clothes.

All boats carried soap which would lather in salt water. Bathing consisted of stripping and jumping into the water while the watch kept a sharp lookout. As soon as you were wet you scrambled on board again, soaped yourself well, and washed off the lather with another quick dive into the briny. Clothes were laundered, using the steel decks as a washboard, and hung up on the jumping wires to dry.

After cleansing both boat and personnel, a good meal was usually prepared, minor repairs made which were considered necessary, and then the boat would be let down gently to the bed of the sea and all hands, save one man left as a guard, would turn in and sleep. So it was these crews lived for long periods, in one particular instance forty-eight days, before they took their lives in their hands again and attempted the passage of the Narrows.

And the food problem was not an easy one to solve. Some cooking could be done on the little electric stoves, but it was impossible to keep good anything that was not hermetically sealed. The submarine owes its development to the diesel engine, the storage battery, and canned goods. Without the latter, none of the endurance exploits of either the British or German submarines would have been possible. Canned goods, hardtack, and the blessedly ubiquitous rum were the chief items on a submarine's menu. Drinking water was a luxury indulged in only when one was really thirsty. After a few weeks out the flavor didn't make it appeal to you even when thirsty. As I have already explained we kept clean in hot weather; there is no need to belabor the fact that we stayed dirty in cold weather. It was impossible to keep dry at any time.

In the Sea of Marmara the crews not only had to be economical with their food and drink, but with their torpedoes and ammunition as well. Every shell had to find a billet, every torpedo its mark. The problem of food and drink was the comparatively simple one of rationing. Perhaps fortunately, the air in a submarine did not induce ravenous appetites. But the problem of guaranteeing each torpedo a bull's-eye was not so simple.

It was the practice in the trade to set all torpedoes to sink if they missed their targets. This prevented their falling into the hands of the enemy or constituting a menace to navigation which would endanger enemy, Allied, and neutral shipping alike. A live torpedo when set to float is nothing more or less than a huge mine and almost as dangerous.

Commander Nasmith agreed that this practice was sensible when a depot ship was handy to supply you with all the "tin fish" you required, but with the Dardanelles between him and fresh supplies he concluded the practice could be modified. He therefore adopted the expedient of setting his torpedoes to float, and, if he missed a shot, he waited until his intended victim had gone on its way, and then

107

retrieved the torpedo at his leisure. "Tin fish which fight and run away must live to fight another day," seems to have been his reading of the old proverb.

The first chance to try this conservation policy came on the twenty-eighth. After sighting a convoy of six ships early in the morning and sinking the largest, he ran in with a steamer bound for Constantinople from Panderma, the railway port on the south shore. The vessel was a long way off, and so located that he couldn't maneuver to get closer. Setting his torpedo to float, he tried the long shot and missed.

E-11 waited until the steamer had disappeared to the north, and prowled around till she found the big cylinder of floating death. The top of the head was grazed but the pistol was not discharged, showing that it had missed the keel by inches. Nasmith was now faced with the problem of getting his torpedo back into its tube. The accepted method was to hoist them aboard from the depot ship by means of a derrick. There was no derrick on *E-11*.

Nasmith blew the water out of her for'ard tanks, and then flooded the after tanks until the boat's bows were raised sufficiently to bring the torpedo tubes just level with the water. The rear doors of the tube inside the boat were then closed, the bow cap opened, and a couple of the crew jumped overboard. Swimming one on either side, they steered the "fish" tail first into its tube. The bow cap was closed, the boat trimmed, water drained from the tube, the rear doors opened; and the torpedo hauled into the for'ard compartment for recharging and overhauling. The new plan had proved itself. It was simple, easily accomplished, and was used successfully a number of times.

To conserve their torpedoes further, Nasmith resorted to other economies. He had no gun, and he disliked wasting precious tin fish on the dhows which were continually plying between the shores of Asia Minor and Turkey in Europe. What he did was to chase them on the surface, come alongside, and force them to surrender. The crew would then be taken aboard *E-11*, and the small sailing boat burned. Another one sighted, the same process would be repeated. When the submarine had collected more passengers than she could accommodate, they were transferred to a captured boat, and a course set for them to the nearest harbor. Occasionally the routine varied. When a fleet of sailing craft was found, the crews were transferred to one of the boats, the rest of the boats tied together and burned. Demolition charges were saved for bigger game. But always the crews were taken care of. Not a single noncombatant lost his life through the operations of our submarines in the Sea of Marmara.

E-11 had now been nine days in and big game was growing very scarce. For two days more she prowled around like a hungry tiger, and found nothing but dhows. These were certainly profitable, and always amusing, but hardly satisfying. As a result, Nasmith dived and proceeded into Panderma Roads. It was here that he found one of the latest vessels of the Rickmers Line, and torpedoed her. She was towed ashore in a sinking condition.

Having received word from the *Jed* of troop movements between Ismid, the port at the eastern tip of the Marmara, and the north shore, *E-11* spent the rest of the day watching the eastern transport route without success, but the very difficulty the boat was experiencing in finding anything to attack was the best possible guarantee of her success.

But June 2 was a big day. After communicating with the *Jed*, *E-11* proceeded toward the northern transport route, and sighted a ship to the eastward. The boat dived, and got in a clean hit on the steamer's port side. The explosion was tremendous. A quivering instant after the torpedo hit, the entire upper deck was lifted overboard. She had been filled with munitions.

An hour later the port-beam tube was fired at a small storeship, and, missing her, ran on toward a small town. The crew of the steamer took her into shore and landed. *E-11* moved in to finish her with a demolition charge, but was driven off by rifle fire. Less than two hours later two destroyers were sighted in company with a dispatch boat. Unseen by the destroyers, a torpedo was sent on its way, and missed. This one was recovered later and passed in through the tubes.

After two comparatively inactive days an examination of the mechanical equipment showed the terrific strain the boat had been under during her seventeen days of gentlemanly raiding. One motor was badly damaged, and one of the driving shafts was cracked. Nasmith thought it advisable to return. June 6 was spent charging batteries and resting, and at 10 P.M. she proceeded as requisite for Gallipoli.

It is hard to imagine that any fitting climax could be managed to round out *E-11*'s cruise. What more astonishing thing was there left her than she had already done? After the tumult in Constantinople it seems that anything must be an anticlimax. But not with Nasmith in command. As I have said of his adventures, each seems a work of art and perfect in its way.

Thanks to her recaptured tin fish, *E-11* still had two loaded tubes. These were being saved for the battleships stationed above the Narrows, which Nasmith was confident of finding on his way out.

Gallipoli was passed at about 100 feet, and *E-11* proceeded toward Nagara, coming up at regular intervals to examine all anchorages for first-class fighting ships. This was to be the climax—the sinking of a Turkish dreadnought.

Slowly she poked her nose down the Dardanelles. Time and again the periscope was raised, swung hopefully through the arc, and drew a blank. Eight miles above Nagara Point a large empty transport was sighted anchored close to shore. Her position was noted and nothing more. The torpedoes were for bigger things. The boat reached Nagara and still nothing had been seen. The three officers were not discouraged. Beyond Nagara, where the straits swing sharply to the south, they would certainly find battleships.

Nagara was passed on their port side, and they, unseen, headed down the narrowing straits toward Chanak and the Narrows. Off Chanak, close to the first minefield, nothing had been seen. At the threshold of escape, with nearly three weeks of astonishing deeds behind her, there seems to have been no question as to what *E-11* should do next. Nasmith ordered the helmsman to turn 16 points, and she doubled back on her track, past Nagara, on to Moussa Bank where the empty transport lay in wait. She was torpedoed, and *E-11* continued her journey down the straits.

With a clear conscience, Nasmith headed for home in earnest. Nothing is mentioned in the boat's official log of the hundred and one dangers she knew she escaped, and the thousand and one dangers she escaped and knew nothing of, but I can remember a member of the crew telling what really happened. It seems to me, knowing submarines, the real climax of the story.

"Just as we got off Kilid Bahr something happened," he told me. "The boat got out of trim. Don't know to this day what got hold of her, but suddenly she started for the surface. Now, we daren't give our position away because patrol craft were as thick as fleas on a dog. Besides, by this time we knew of the torpedo tubes they had rigged up ashore on both sides of the Narrows, and we also knew they had set observation mines which they could explode from the shore if they got one glimpse of our periscope as we made our way through.

"As I say, I don't know what happened to make her rise, but we had to flood every tank in her to keep from breaking surface. It may have been a sudden change in the density of the water, it may have been anything, but no sooner had we got her down and under control again, than she did just the opposite and started to take a dive. She was down to depths greater than her builders ever intended her to go before we got the ballast water out of her and started coming up again."

Having extracted themselves from this delicate situation, they next heard a noise as though they had grounded. This was impossible when no bottom was near. There was nothing for it but to find out the cause of the grating, and the boat was brought up to 20 feet. The periscope was raised—reluctantly enough, I should say. As soon as the periscope was clear an ominous bulk was seen pushing on ahead. A mine had evidently fouled on their for'ard port hydroplane.

No less welcome companion could be imagined. A roll, a lurch, a slip in the fouled chain, and one of the delicate horns would have made contact. They dared not come to the surface to disengage it because of the batteries ashore, and so they proceeded pushing the engine of death ahead of them until they got as far as Kum Kale. For well over an hour the crew lived an exquisite nightmare expecting some one of the crawling seconds to be the last they would ever know.

Outside the entrance to the straits Nasmith undertook the infinitely delicate task of clearing her. First he emptied his after tanks, which allowed her bows to sink. Then he ordered full speed astern on the motors. In this position the boat rose to the surface. The sternway gathered and the rush of water from the screws swept the mine away from her bows.

Shortly after, she was met by the British destroyer *Grampus* and escorted into Mudros. In addition to the moral effect of her cruise, she had sunk two ammunition ships, two storeships, two troopships, a number of sailing vessels, and beached a third transport with a gaping hole in her.

As in the case of Holbrook and Boyle, Lieutenant-Commander Nasmith received the Victoria Cross, and his officers and crew were proportionately decorated.

*Comdr. J. Valerio Borghese, commanding officer of the Italian sub-
marine* Scirè, *describes in this story one of World War II's greatest
midget submarine attacks. Comparatively speaking, the Italian U-
boats were not overly successful, but for pure courage, the feat of
the midget crews' attack on British ships* Valiant *and* Queen Elizabeth *at Alexandria has seldom been equaled.*

This story begins as the Scirè *is approaching the entrance to Alexandria Harbor.*

Target: Battleships!

J. VALERIO BORGHESE

THE plan of operations provided for the arrival of the *Scirè* on a certain evening, a few thousand meters from the entrance to Alexandria
Harbor; as it was assumed that everything would be in darkness
(owing to the blackout), it had been arranged that, in order to facili-
tate the submarine's landfall, the coast being low-lying and without
conspicuous features, and to allow her to identify the harbor (for
the success of the operators' raid would depend largely on the precision with which the point of their release was determined), on the
evening before, and also on the one of the action, our aircraft would
bomb the harbor. The submarine would then release the operators.
The latter, proceeding on courses laid down beforehand, as soon as
they arrived in front of the harbor, would have to overcome the
obstructions and attack the targets previously assigned to them by
the commander of the *Scirè*, who would base his orders on the latest
data transmitted to him by radio. After attaching the charges to the
hulls of the targets, the operators were to lay a certain number of
floating incendiary bombs with which they had been supplied. These
bombs would go off about an hour after the warheads had exploded
and were intended to set alight the oil which would by then have
spread from the ships which had been attacked; it was expected that
this would cause fire to break out in the harbor, affecting all the
vessels therein, together with the floating docks, the harbor installa-

113

tions, and the warehouses . . . ; thus putting the chief enemy naval base in the eastern Mediterranean utterly out of action.

The *Scirè*, directly the operators had been dropped, was to start back. The pilots had been told which zones of the interior of the harbor were considered the least vigilantly watched, where they were to land on conclusion of the operation, and what routes they were to take to get clear of the harbor area in the shortest possible time. Plans had also been laid for their rescue: on the days following the action, the submarine *Zaffiro* (commanded by Giovanni Lombardi) would shuttle for two consecutive nights 10 miles off Rosetta in the Nile Delta; such operators as eluded immediate capture would be able to reach her by any boat they could find on the coast.

The *Scirè*, with the pilots aboard, left Leros on the morning of the fourteenth. She proceeded without incident and, so to speak, in secret; by day we submerged, surfacing only at night, to charge the batteries and freshen up the atmosphere aboard. The task of the *Scirè* was, as usual, to find a method of getting as close as possible to the enemy harbor, without arousing prohibitive alarm or allowing her presence to be suspected. Discovery would mean arousing antisubmarine measures; a remorseless pursuit would begin, which would prevent us from carrying out the operation. We therefore took the strictest precautions. And as we might be detected by hydrophones as a result of normal sounds aboard the submarine, we had to proceed noiselessly, muffling the machinery. The intelligence we had received on setting out was to the effect that Alexandria Harbor was surrounded, like all other harbors in time of war, by minefields. To quote the report: *"Fixed and mobile defenses ascertained: (a)* minefield 20 miles NW of harbor; *(b)* line of 'lobster pots' arranged at a depth of 30 fathoms in a circle with a radius of about 6 miles; *(c)* line of detector cables closer in; *(d)* groups of 'lobster pots' in known positions; *(e)* net barriers relatively easy to force; *(f)* advanced observation line beyond minefield."

How could all these dangers be circumvented? How could the minefields be evaded if we did not know the security routes? Or the "lobster pots"? Or the detector cables?

In order to reach the target we were obliged, after a certain stage, to trust to luck; there was nothing else to do. But luck can be "assisted," especially when the matter in hand is a complex one. I had therefore decided that, as soon as we reached a depth of 400 meters

114

(which would probably be where the minefields started), we would proceed at a depth of not less than 60 meters, since I assumed that the mines, even if they were antisubmarine, would be located at a higher level; if the submarine should then collide with one of the mooring cables, I felt sure that the latter would slide along her sides, which were accurately streamlined and carefully cleared of all adherent matter, without getting caught up anywhere, till it fell harmlessly astern. There was nothing else I could do to elude the peril of the mines, except, naturally, to trust to luck.

The other difficulty was that of taking the submarine to the *precise* point prearranged; in other words, to navigate with the exactitude of a draftsman working with compass and ruler, despite the drifting caused by underwater currents, which are always difficult to deal with, and despite, above all, the impossibility of ascertaining one's position from the moment when, at dawn of the day appointed for the operation, the submarine would be obliged to submerge (so as not to be detected from the enemy base) and proceed at a great depth (to avoid mines), until the time came to release the operators.

The solution of this problem of underwater navigation cannot be reached without perfect control of the speed of the vessel; the course has to be laid and kept to with great precision (so as to eliminate errors due to faulty steering) and finally position has to be determined from variations in depth quota, the only hydrographic factor which can be ascertained in a submerged submarine; here we are in a sphere closer to that of art than to the science of navigation.

Everyone aboard gave me effective help, officers, petty officers and seamen. Each man, in his own special department, took care that his services should be regularly maintained and that his machinery should function in such a way as to prevent any unforeseen accident which might compromise the success of the operation.

Ursano, my second-in-command, had the general supervision of routine aboard; Benini and Olcese, the two efficient navigation officers, helped me in following the course and with the tricky business of dealing with codes and communication; while Tajer, the chief engineer, regulated the performance of the machinery (engines, electric batteries, air supply, etc.) and kept the respective services in order. The petty officers were first-rate: Ravera was chief mechanic, Farina chief torpedo gunner, and Rapetti chief electrician; the wireless operators kept us in continuous touch with Rome and Athens;

all were praiseworthy in the discharge of their various duties. Last but not least, there was the cook (a seaman to whom this task had been allotted; he was a mason in civil life) who became the martyr aboard; he was on his feet 24 hours out of 24 at the tiny, red-hot electric stoves, whatever the sea was like, concocting from dry rations dishes to satisfy the tastes and digestions of sixty people, as well as hot drinks for those on night watch and solid meals to keep up the spirits of the operators.

The latter, meanwhile, in perfect serenity (for the die was now cast) stored up their energy by resting. De la Penne, with his big fair head of rumpled hair, was generally to be found lying in his bunk asleep. Even as he slumbered he would every now and then stretch out an arm, put his hand into a drawer and extract a large fruitcake, which he ate up at a great rate. Then he would blissfully turn over and go back to his dreams.

Martellotta, permanently in good spirits, occupied another bunk. "Peace and good will!" was his invariable greeting; a heartening phrase. Marceglia, a giant of a man, with a tranquil temperament and something stately about him, was absorbed in study: his *basso profundo* tones were rarely heard and, when they were, it was to make some technical request or utter some comment on the operation. Feltrinelli, Bianchi, Marino, Schergat, Favale, and Memoli all managed to find acceptable accommodation among the ship's equipment and spent their days in unbroken repose, only interrupted for the necessary more-than-substantial meals.

Public health was in the hands of Spaccarelli, surgeon, diver, and reserve crew leader; every day he put the pilots through a thorough medical examination; it was essential to have them in the pink of condition on the day of the operation, which was now at hand.

The pilots remained very calm: the difficulties and dangers of which they were naturally well aware did not make them uneasy but merely increased their determination; anxiety and strain were inevitable, but did not find expression; talk went on at the ordinary level of cheerful tranquillity characteristic of life aboard; there were periods of gay hilarity, when facetious repartees were exchanged.

They were really extraordinary fellows, those lads; they were about to undertake action which would require the exploitation of their whole physical and moral energy and put their lives in peril at every moment, hour after hour; it would be a mission from which,

116

at best, they could only hope to emerge as prisoners of war, and yet they preserved the attitude of a team of sportsmen off to play their customary Sunday game.

Meanwhile the *Scirè* encountered, on December 16, a heavy storm.

"In order to avoid exposing materials, and above all our operators, to excessive strain, I remained submerged even at night, the moment our supplies of air and electricity had been taken in."

The same day I wrote:

"In consequence of the bad weather and the lack of exact information as to the number and size of the enemy units in harbor, I decided to postpone the operation for 24 hours from the night of the 17th/18th to that of the 18th/19th." (From my official report.)

On December 17, I added:

"In view of the ship's position and the favorable weather conditions I decided that the operation should take place on the evening of the 18th, hoping that I should meanwhile receive precise intelligence regarding the presence of vessels in harbor."

This was a hope that was soon realized. The same evening we obtained at last, to our great delight, confirmation from Athens that both battleships were at Alexandria.

The word was now: forward! Throughout the day, on the eighteenth, the *Scirè* proceeded through a zone which we presumed to be mined, at a depth of 60 meters, over bottoms which rose rapidly as we approached the coast, till we slipped over them like a silent and invisible tank, "continually regulating our movements in accordance with the rise of the seabed, till at 1840 hours we found ourselves at the prearranged point, 1.3 miles by 356° from the lighthouse at the west mole of the commercial harbor of Alexandria, at a depth of 15 meters."

Preparations were made for release of the operators. As soon as I had discovered, by a survey taken through the periscope, that the darkness was complete, I surfaced just sufficiently to enable the trap-

117

door to be opened ("outcrop level," as it is technically known) and came out on the conning tower. The weather was perfect: it was pitch dark; the sea very smooth and the sky unclouded. Alexandria was right ahead of me, very close. I identified some of its characteristic buildings and determined my position; to my great satisfaction I found that we were within a meter of the prearranged point. This was an exceptional result after sixteen hours of blind navigation! Immediately afterwards, with the pilots wrapped in their rubber suits and wearing their breathing sets, the ceremony of leave-taking began; we neither spoke nor embraced one another: "Commander," was all they said, "give us the good-luck kick, will you?" And with this strange rite, into which I put all I knew, so that my good wishes might be evident, the farewell ceremony terminated.

The first to go up were the two leaders of the reserve crews, Feltrinelli and Spaccarelli. Their job was to open the cylinder doors, to save the operators the fatigue of doing so.

One by one, de la Penne and Bianchi, Marceglia and Schergat, Martellotta and Marino, covered from head to foot in their black suits, their movements encumbered by their breathing gear, went up the ladder and disappeared into the darkness of the night and the sea. I submerged to the bottom.

A few minutes later the hydrophones told us that the three crews were on their way. "God be with them," I prayed, "and speed them well!"

Inside the submarine we waited for the sounds of blows struck against the deck, the agreed signal to be made when the doors of the cylinders, now empty, had been closed and the reserves were ready to be taken aboard again. When at last we heard them, I surfaced. Feltrinelli told me, in a voice broken by emotion, that as he could see no sign of Spaccarelli, he had gone astern to look for him: by pure chance he had stumbled against something soft on deck; he had discovered by groping (for we must not forget that the scene took place underwater at night) that it was the missing Spaccarelli, who seemed lifeless. I instantly sent up two other divers, who had been kept ready for any emergency; Spaccarelli was lifted up and lowered down the ladder into the interior of the submarine. I descended to the bottom again and began to head for home, following precisely the same course which had proved to be safe during my approach.

The unfortunate Spaccarelli was forthwith relieved of his mask, breathing set, and diver's suit and put to bed; he was quite blue in the face, his pulse was imperceptible, and he was not breathing; he showed every normal symptom of having been drowned.

What was to be done? The mission's surgeon was not much use to us in this extremity, for he himself was the victim. I arranged for two men to give him continuous artificial respiration; I rummaged in the medicine chest and had him injected with the contents of all the phials that, judging from the description of the ingredients, seemed capable of exercising a stimulating action on the heart and circulation; others gave him oxygen (the air aboard was emphatically unsuitable in this case); all the resources of our extremely slender store of medicaments and of our still slenderer knowledge of medicine were brought into play in the attempt to achieve what appeared to be an utter impossibility, the resuscitation of a dead man.

Meanwhile the *Scirè*, with this dramatic episode taking place aboard her, slipped along the seabed, farther and farther away from Alexandria. We took care not to reveal our presence in any way; discovery would have been fatal to the six adventurous lads who were at that very moment engaged in the crucial phase of the operation. But the submarine was not responding very well to my directions: the cylinder doors astern had been left open, a circumstance which made it difficult for me to keep my depth and maintain trim. As soon as we were some miles from the coast I surfaced to close them. I noticed that the Ras el Tin Lighthouse was functioning; a number of lights which I had not seen before showed at the entrance to the harbor; units were evidently going in or out; I hoped the operators would be able to take advantage of the fact. As for the cylinders, I found that they could not be closed on account of damage to one of the doors.

I continued on my course of withdrawal, remaining submerged, for the zone we were now crossing had been notified as constituting the minefield. After three and a half hours' continuous artificial respiration, a number of injections, and some applications of oxygen, our surgeon, who had till then shown not the smallest sign of life, drew his first wheezing breath; it was a deep, hoarse sound, resembling a death rattle. But it meant he was alive and we could save him! A few hours later, in fact, though his condition was still serious, he got back the use of his voice and was able to tell us that while he was making a terrific effort to close the starboard cylinder door, which stubbornly resisted every attempt he made, the effects of the oxygen he was breathing and those of water pressure at the depth involved had caused him to faint; luckily he fell on deck and did not slip overboard, as might very easily have happened, for there were no rails or bulwarks to the vessel (they had been removed to prevent the mine-cables from catching on them).

At last, on the evening of the nineteenth, since we were now presumably clear of the minefields, the *Scirè* surfaced, after 39 hours of submersion, and set course for Leros. On the evening of the twentieth we received the following wireless communication from the Naval Supreme Command: "Photographic reconnaissance indicates two battleships hit." There was great enthusiasm aboard; no one had doubted it would be a success, but to have our expectations confirmed so soon gave us great satisfaction.

On the evening of the twenty-first, as soon as we had docked at Port Lago, we took Spaccarelli ashore to the local naval hospital. He was now out of danger but still required a good deal of attention in consequence of the severe shock he had experienced.

The return of the *Scirè* from Leros to La Spezia proceeded without any notable incidents, except that on Christmas Day, while the submarine was off Bengasi and the crew were listening to the Pope's speech on the loudspeaker, an aircraft of unidentified nationality came a little too close to the vessel and got within range of our four 13.2 machine guns; the natural retaliation was the dropping of five bombs about 80 meters astern of us, which did no damage. Our Christmas pies!

On December 29, the *Scirè* arrived at La Spezia. Admiral Bacci, now chief of the North Tyrrhenian Sector, was waiting for us on the pier; he brought us greetings and congratulations from Admiral Riccardi, Undersecretary of State for the Navy.

I was glad of this tribute to my gallant crew, who had worked so hard, with such efficiency and courage, in bringing our submarine back to harbor after 27 days of operational service, 22 of them at sea, and had covered without mishap 3,500 miles, thus contributing to a great victory for Italy.

How had it fared with the operators, whom we had left in the open sea, outside Alexandria Harbor, astride their fragile torpedoes, plunged beneath the waves in the darkness of night, surrounded by enemies in ambush? The three crews had left the submarine in company and commenced approach along the prearranged routes.

The sea was very calm, the night dark. Lights in the harbor permitted the pilots to determine their position, which they found to be precisely as planned. They went ahead so coolly that at one point, as de la Penne relates in his report, "As we were ahead of schedule, we opened our ration tins and had a meal. We were then 500 meters from the Ras el Tin Lighthouse."

At last they reached the net defenses at the harbor's entrance.

"We saw some people at the end of the pier and heard them talking; one of them was walking about with a lighted oil-lamp.

"We also saw a large motorboat cruising in silence off the pier and dropping depth charges. These charges were rather a nuisance to us."

While the six heads, only just above water, were looking, with all the concentrated attention of which they were capable, for a gap in the net, three British destroyers suddenly appeared at the entrance to the harbor, waiting to go in; guide lights were switched on to show them the way and the net gates were thrown wide open. Without a second's hesitation, our three assault craft slipped into the harbor with the British destroyers: they were in! They had lost sight of one another during this maneuver, but they were now close to their targets. The latter had been distributed as follows: de la Penne was to take the battleship *Valiant*, Marceglia the battleship *Queen Elizabeth*, and Martellotta was to look for the aircraft carrier; if she were not in harbor, he was to attack a loaded tanker in the hope that the oil or petrol which would issue from it would spread over the water and thus furnish excellent fuel for the floating incendiary bombs the operators were to scatter before abandoning their "pigs."

We will now take up the stories of the individual crews.

De la Penne—Bianchi. Inside the harbor, after passing the interned French warships, the presence of which was well known, de la Penne sighted, at the presumed anchorage, the huge dark mass of the target assigned to him, the 32,000-ton battleship *Valiant*. As he approached her, he encountered the antitorpedo net barrier; he got through it *surfaced* "in order to lose as little time as possible, for I found that my physical condition, owing to the cold, would be unlikely to let me hold out much longer." (His diver's suit had been

121

leaking ever since he had left the submarine.) He had no difficulty with negotiation of the net; he was now 30 meters from the *Valiant*; it was nineteen minutes past two. He touched the hull, giving it a slight bump; in performing the evolution necessary to get beneath the hull, his "pig" seemed to take on extra weight and went to the bottom in 17 meters of water; de la Penne dived after it and discovered to his amazement that there was no sign of his second pilot. He rose to the surface to look for him, but could not see him; everything was quiet aboard the battleship; no alarm had been given. De la Penne left Bianchi to his fate, returned to the bottom, and tried to start the engine of his craft to get it underneath the hull, as it had meanwhile moved some distance away. But the engine would not start; a rapid check-over soon showed what the trouble was: a steel wire had got entangled in the propeller.

What was to be done? All alone, with his craft immobilized on the seabed a few meters from the target, de la Penne resolved to try the only possible expedient: this was to drag the "pig" by main force, finding his direction from the compass, beneath the battleship. Speed was essential, for he feared that at any moment the British might pick up his second pilot, who had probably fainted and would be floating about close by . . . ; the alarm would be given, depth charges would be dropped, his operation and those of his companions would be doomed to certain failure, for they would be at work only a few hundred meters away. With all his strength, panting and sweating, he dragged at the craft; his goggles became obscured and the mud he was stirring up prevented his reading the compass, his breath began to come in great gasps and it became difficult to breathe at all through the mask, but he stuck to it and made progress; he could hear, close above him, the noises made aboard the ship, especially the sound of an alternating pump, which he used to find his direction. After forty minutes of superhuman effort, making a few inches at every pull, he at last bumped his head against the hull. He made a cursory survey of the position: he seemed to be at about the middle of the ship, an excellent spot for causing maximum damage. He was now almost exhausted; but he used the last vestiges of his strength to set the time fuses; in accordance with the orders he had received, he regulated them so as to cause the explosion at five o'clock precisely (Italian time, corresponding with six o'clock local time). He did not release his incendiary bombs, for when they rose to the surface they would reveal the presence and the position of the threat now established under the hull with the fuses in action. He left his craft on the seabed under the vessel and swam to the surface. The moment he got his head above water he removed his mask and sank it; the fresh, pure air revived him; he began to swim slowly away from the ship. But someone called out to him, a searchlight picked him out, a burst of machine-gun fire brought him to a halt. He swam back toward the vessel and climbed out of the water on to the mooring buoy at the bows of the *Valiant*. He found there his second pilot Bianchi, who, after fainting, had risen to the surface like a balloon and on regaining consciousness had hidden himself on the buoy so as not to risk causing an alarm which would have disturbed the work of his leader. "Aboard they were making facetious remarks, believing that our operation had failed; they were talking contemptuously about Italians. I called Bianchi's attention to the probability that in a few hours they would have changed their minds about the Italians." It was then about 3:30. At last a motorboat turned up and the two "shipwrecked" men were picked up by it and taken aboard the battleship. A British officer asked who they were, where they had come from, and expressed ironical sympathy with their lack of success. The two operators, who were now prisoners of war, made clear who they were, by handing over their military identity cards. They refused to answer any other questions. They were taken in the motorboat, separated from each other, to a hut ashore, near the Ras el Tin Lighthouse. Bianchi was the first to be cross-examined; on leaving the hut he made a sign to de la Penne indicating that he had said nothing. It was then the latter's turn: naturally, he held his tongue; the Britisher, who had a revolver in his hand, seemed to be an excitable sort of fellow; "I'll soon find a way to make you talk," he said, in excellent Italian. The men were taken back aboard the *Valiant;* it was then four o'clock.

They were received by the commanding officer, Captain Morgan, who asked them where the charge was located. On their refusing to answer, the two men, accompanied by the officer of the watch and escorted by an armed picket, were placed in one of the holds forward, between the two gun turrets, not very far from the point at which the charge would explode.

We will now let de la Penne take up the tale.

123

"Our escorts were rather white about the gills and behaved very nicely to us; they gave me rum to drink and offered me cigarettes; they also tried to make us talk. Bianchi sat down and went to sleep. I perceived from the ribbons on the sailors' caps that we were aboard the battleship *Valiant*. When there were about ten minutes left before the explosion, I asked if I could speak to the commanding officer. I was taken aft, into his presence. I told him that in a few minutes his ship would blow up, that there was nothing he could do about it and that, if he wished, he could still get his crew into a place of safety. He again asked me where I had placed the charge and as I did not reply had me escorted back to the hold. As we went along I heard the loudspeakers giving orders to abandon ship, as the vessel had been attacked by Italians, and saw people running aft. When I was again in the hold I said to Bianchi, as I came down the ladder, that things had turned out badly and that it was all up with us, but that we could be content, since we had succeeded, in spite of everything, in bringing the operation to a successful conclusion. Bianchi, however, did not answer me. I looked for him and could not find him. I supposed that the British, believing that I had confessed, had removed him. A few minutes passed (they were infernal ones for me: would the explosion take place?) and then it came. The vessel reared, with extreme violence. All the lights went out and the hold became filled with smoke. I was surrounded by shackles which had been hanging from the ceiling and had now fallen. I was unhurt, except for pain in a knee, which had been grazed by one of the shackles in its fall. The vessel was listing to port. I opened one of the portholes very near sea level, hoping to be able to get through it and escape. This proved to be impossible, as the porthole was too small, and I gave up the idea; but I left the port open, hoping that through it more water would enter. I waited for a few moments. The hold was now illuminated by the light which entered through the port. I concluded that it would be rash to stay there any longer, noticing that the vessel was now lying on the bottom and continuing slowly to list to port. I climbed up the ladder and, finding the hatchway open, began to walk aft; there was no one about. But there were still many of the crew at the stern. They got up as I

124

passed them; I went on till I reached the captain. At that moment he was engaged in giving orders for salvaging his ship. I asked him what he had done with my diver. He did not reply and the officer of the watch told me to be silent. The ship had now listed through 4–5 degrees and come to a standstill. I saw from a clock that it was a quarter past six. I went further aft, where a number of officers were standing, and began to watch the battleship *Queen Elizabeth,* which lay about 500 meters astern of us.

"The crew of that battleship were standing in her bows. A few seconds passed and then the *Queen Elizabeth,* too, blew up. She rose a few inches out of the water and fragments of iron and other objects flew out of her funnel, mixed with oil which even reached the deck of the *Valiant,* splashing every one of us standing on her stern. An officer came up and asked me to tell him on my word of honor if there were any other charges under the ship. I made no reply and was then again taken back to the hold. After about a quarter of an hour I was escorted up to the officers' mess, where at last I could sit down, and where I found Bianchi. Shortly afterwards I was put aboard a motorboat, which took me back to Ras el Tin.

"I noticed that the anchor, which had been hanging at the bows, was now underwater. During transit an officer asked me whether we had got in through the gaps in the mole. At Ras el Tin we were locked in two cells and kept there until toward evening. I asked whether I could be given a little sunlight, as I was again very cold. A soldier came, felt my pulse and told me that I was perfectly all right.

"Toward evening we were put into a small lorry and transported therein to a prisoner of war camp in Alexandria. I found some Italians in the camp who had heard the explosions that morning. We lay down on the ground, without having had any food, and, though we were soaked through, we slept till the following morning. I was taken to the infirmary for treatment of my knee injury and some Italian orderlies gave me an excellent dish of macaroni. The next morning I was removed to Cairo." (From the report handed in by Lt. Luigi de la Penne on his return from prison.)

In 1944, after de la Penne and Bianchi had come back to Italy from prison, they were awarded the gold medal for gallantry in war. And he who pinned the medal on the chest of de la Penne was none other than Admiral Morgan, formerly commanding officer of the *Valiant* and at that time chief of the Allied naval mission in Italy.

Marceglia–Schergat. Approach commenced in company with de la Penne on the prearranged course. About midnight they saw the guide lights at the entrance to the harbor switched on; it was clear that units were either going in or coming out. Violent shocks were felt against the casing of the "pig," as though it had crashed against some metallic obstacle, accompanied by strong contraction of the leg muscles of the pilots: these were the effects of depth charges dropped by the enemy at the entrance to the harbor to prevent "unwelcome visits." As they slipped into the entrance channel they noticed, much to their surprise and satisfaction, that the net gates had been opened. Shortly afterwards, toward one o'clock, they had to take rapid evasive action to avoid being run down by three destroyers which were just coming in. Marceglia resumed the prearranged course: "In no time at all I found myself face to face with the whole massive bulk of my target." He came upon the antitorpedo net, got through it, and, now that the way was clear, submerged beneath the hull, in line with the funnel. With the aid of his second pilot, Marceglia precisely carried out the maneuver: he clamped a loop line connecting the two bilge keels and attached the warhead of his torpedo to the central point of the line, so that it hung about a meter and a half below the hull; then he set the fuse in motion. It was then 3:15 A.M. (Italian time).

"I tried to analyze my sensations at that moment. I found that I did not feel particularly thrilled, but only rather tired and just starting to get cold. We got astride our craft again: my diver made me urgent signs to surface, as he was just about all in. I pumped in air to surface; the craft only detached itself from the bottom with difficulty, then at last it started to rise, at first slowly, later more rapidly. So as not to burst out of the water too suddenly, I had to exhaust; the air bubbles attracted the attention of the watch aft. He switched on a searchlight and we surfaced right into its rays. We ducked down on the craft to make the target as small as possible and prevent our goggles from reflecting the light. Shortly afterwards the searchlight was switched off; we started on our return, which took us past the bows of the ship; a man was walking up and down the fo'c'sle deck, I could see his cigarette glowing; everything was quiet aboard. We got out of the obstructed zone and, at last, took off our masks; it was very cold; I couldn't prevent my teeth chattering. We stopped again and began distributing our incendiaries after setting the fuses." (From a report by Engineer Captain Antonio Marceglia.)

They then set off for the spot on which they were to land: it was the area which, according to our maps and intelligence reports, was the least strictly guarded and furnished the most convenient access to the city.

While still some distance from land they set going the fuse of the craft's self-destructor and sank her; they swam ashore, removed their breathing sets and rubber suits, cut everything to pieces and buried the strips under the rocks. Then they waded ashore: it was 4:30 A.M.; they had been in the water exactly eight hours.

Marceglia and Schergat succeded in leaving the harbor area unobserved. Posing as French sailors, they entered the city of Alexandria; after wandering about for some time, they made their way to the station to take the train for Rosetta and try to rejoin the submarine which would be lying about 10 miles out to sea at certain prearranged times, a night or two later. But at this point their troubles began: the sterling with which they were supplied did not circulate in Egypt; they wasted a lot of time trying to get it changed and were not able to leave until the evening. At Rosetta they spent the night in a squalid little inn, hiding from frequent visits by the police; next day, in the evening, they made for the seashore, but were stopped by the Egyptian police, recognized as Italians, and turned over to the British naval authorities.

Their attempt to evade capture was thus frustrated.

Marceglia's operation may be characterized as a "perfect" one, meaning by this phrase that it was performed without a hitch at every stage and nothing unforeseen happened. In a letter he wrote me some years later he observed: "As you can see, sir, our performance had nothing heroic about it; its success was due solely to the preparations made, the specially favorable conditions under which it took place, and above all the determination to succeed at all costs."

Preparations, determination, and luck were rewarded with the gold medal for gallantry in war, which both Marceglia and Schergat obtained on their release from prison.

Martellotta—Marino. Martellotta writes in his report:

"Aboard the submarine *Scirè* at 1630 on December 18, 1941, I received from Lieutenant Commander Borghese the following operational orders: 'Attack to be made on a large loaded tanker and six incendiaries to be distributed in its immediate neighborhood.'

"The presence of twelve loaded tankers in harbor at Alexandria, with a total tonnage of 120,000, was sufficient indication of the importance of the order received: the fire which might be started would be capable of reaching such proportions as to bring about the entire destruction of the harbor itself, with all the units present and all the shore installations.

"Nevertheless, I felt obliged to reply: 'Sir, I shall obey your orders; but I should like you to know that my diver and I would rather have attacked a warship.'

"The captain smiled at this remark of mine and, to please me, since he was aware that there was a possibility of an aircraft carrier having returned to the harbor, he modified the original operational orders to read: 'Search to be made for the aircraft carrier at its two normal anchorages and attack to be made on it if found; otherwise, all other targets consisting of active war units to be ignored and a large loaded tanker to be attacked with distribution of the six incendiaries in its immediate neighborhood.' "

Martellotta had a certain amount of trouble in opening the door of the cylinder and asked Spaccarelli to help him (this was the difficulty which involved Spaccarelli in the adventure related above); he finally joined the other two crews and continued approach in their company as far as the entrance net gate.

"I felt shocks from depth charges and violent pressure against my legs, as though they were being crushed against the craft

128

by some heavy object. I put on my mask and, so as to avoid injury from the frequent shocks being inflicted at vulnerable parts of my body, I ducked in such a way as to lie low in the water, but with heart, lungs, and head above the surface. I told Marino, my diver, to put on his mask also and to take up a similar position, but facing aft, since I was unable myself to keep an eye open in that direction, engaged as I was in looking ahead and having only the limited area of visibility which the mask allowed.

"We arrived in these positions at the entrance to the harbor . . . We did not find obstructions, as we had expected, at the pierheads: the channel was clear.

"We went ahead very slowly. Suddenly, my diver, Marino, thumped me on the shoulder and said: 'Hard a-starboard.' I instantly swerved in the direction indicated, putting on speed, but the craft struck the buoys of the fixed interior barrier, being driven against them by the waves from the bow of a ship which had caught me up as it entered the harbor. It was a destroyer, showing no lights and going at about 10 knots; I distinctly heard chains clashing at her bows and saw members of the crew on deck getting ready to moor. It was then 0030 hours on December 19. I got going again and, taking advantage of the waves made by a second destroyer as it entered the harbor, I slipped in with it, still surfaced and passing within about 20 meters of the guardship."

Martellotta, therefore, was now inside the harbor; he started looking for the aircraft carrier at its two habitual anchorages; he could not find her (as a matter of fact she was not in harbor that night). But he did sight a large warship; believing her to be a battleship, he initiated attack; he had already got under her hull when he discovered that she was, on the contrary, a cruiser and with great reluctance, in obedience to orders received, abandoned the attack; just as he was clearing her after davits he was caught in the rays of a pocket torch aboard her; some seconds of utter immobility ensued, during which he felt as if even his heart had stopped beating; then the torch went out. He made for the zone of the tankers. Martellotta was now beginning to notice signs of strain: his head ached and he had to vomit; he could no longer keep the mouthpiece of the mask

129

between his lips; he took it off and went ahead surfaced. There were the tankers. "I sighted a large one, heavily loaded, which I guessed to be about 16,000 tons." Not being able to submerge, he decided to carry out the attack from the surface: while Martellotta kept the "pig" under the stern of the tanker, the second pilot, Marino, fastened the charge beneath the hull. By 2:55 the fuse had been set going. While this operation was proceeding, a smaller tanker had come alongside the one under attack.

"When Marino rose to the surface and saw her, he said: 'Let's hope she stays here another three hours and then she'll have her hash settled too.' Next, we started off again, for distribution of the incendiaries: we moored them, after setting their fuses, about 100 meters from the tanker and 20 meters apart."

The operation having been carried out in detail so far, the final stage began: this would be the attempt to escape so as not to fall into the hands of the enemy. They got ashore at the agreed place without incident, destroyed, by way of preventive action, their breathing sets and divers' suits and sank the "pig" after setting the self-destructor fuse. Then they went ashore.

"I set off with Marino to get clear of the harbor zone and enter the city: we were stopped at a control point and arrested by some Egyptian customs officials and police, who summoned a second lieutenant and six privates of the British marines. We were taken to an office occupied by two lieutenants of the Egyptian police, who started cross-examining us; while I was answering the questions put to me in as evasive and vague a manner as I could, a British naval commander arrived and requested the senior of the two Egyptian officers to hand us over to the British. The Egyptian refused to do so in the absence of any authority from his government, pointing out that, as he had found us to be Italians from the documents we carried, and Egypt was not at war with Italy, he would have to get special instructions.

"The British commander, after obtaining the necessary authorization from his admiral, made a personal application to the Egyptian government for the instructions required and succeeded in getting us handed over.

"My waterproof watch was on the table with the other articles taken possession of and I never took my eyes off it. Shortly after 5:54 A.M. a violent explosion was heard, which shook the whole building. A few minutes later, as we were getting into a car to follow the British officer, a second explosion was heard, farther away, and after the car had started, a third. At the Ras el Tin naval headquarters we were briefly interrogated, courteously enough, and then dispatched to the concentration camp for prisoners of war at Cairo." (From the report of Gunner Captain Vincenzo Martellotta.)

Martellotta and Marino, on their release from captivity, were also awarded the gold medal for gallantry in war.

The Italian War Bulletin N. 585 of January 8, 1942, gives the following account of the success of the operation:

"On the night of December 18 assault craft of the Italian Royal Navy entered the harbor of Alexandria and attacked two British battleships anchored there. It has only just been confirmed that a battleship of the *Valiant* class was seriously damaged and put into dock for repairs, and is still there."

The following Bulletin, N. 586 of January 9, rounds off the information as follows:

"In the operation conducted by assault craft of the Italian Royal Navy in the harbor of Alexandria and reported in yesterday's Bulletin we now have definite further intelligence that, in addition to the *Valiant*, a second battleship of the *Barham* class was also damaged."

Such was the modest announcement of a naval victory unparalleled throughout the war for precision of execution and importance of strategic results. At the cost of six men captured, there had been sunk, in addition to a large tanker, two 32,000-ton battleships, the last of those at the disposal of the British in the Mediterranean. Crippled by the charges applied to their hulls by the daring members of the Tenth Light Flotilla, the vessels were at a later date, after much expenditure of energy and materials, refloated, patched up for the time being, and then transferred to quiet and distant yards for refit; but they made no further contribution to the war and immediately after the cessation of hostilities they were removed for demolition.

The losses of the *Valiant* and the *Queen Elizabeth,* following those of the *Ark Royal* and the *Barham* in the Mediterranean and almost contemporaneous with the destruction of the *Repulse* and the extremely recent *Prince of Wales* in Indonesia at the hands of Japanese aviators, brought about a most critical situation for the British navy, which was only retrieved after a long lapse of time and then only by means of American assistance.

The strategic position in the Mediterranean was now reversed: for the first (and last) time in the course of the war the Italian navy achieved crushing superiority and dominated the Mediterranean; it could therefore resume, with practical immunity, supplies to the armies overseas and carry out transport of the German *Afrika Corps* to Libya, thus causing the defeat, a few months later, of the British army, which was driven out of Cyrenaica.

Even more could have been done: Italy's naval superiority at that time was such as to permit her armed forces to undertake a direct attack against the pivot of the war in the Mediterranean (and perhaps not only in that theater of war), namely, Malta. An invasion force transported by a convoy protected by the entire Italian fleet, when our battleships would be opposed by *no* such British vessels, would have eliminated that obstacle in the heart of the Mediterranean, which had done us so much harm already and was to do us even more later on. Such an operation would have disposed of the difficulties which the Italian navy had to encounter, for months afterwards, in supplying our African army.

In view of the disproportion between naval forces, the operation would certainly have succeeded, though it might have been accompanied by serious losses. When the thorn in the flank of Italy's line of communication across the Mediterranean had thus been eliminated, the occupation of Egypt would only have been a question of time, bringing with it incalculable consequences for the outcome of the war.

The responsibility for losing this opportunity rests, in my opinion, on the Italian general staff and, still more, upon the German high command which, by refusing to supply the necessary fuel for our warships and aircraft, "again displayed its underestimation of sea power in the general conduct of the war and in particular of the importance of the Mediterranean in the general picture of the entire conflict." (From the report of Admiral Weichold, a German liaison officer attached to the Italian Supreme Naval Command, submitted to the Anglo-Americans after the war.)

The great victory at Alexandria was therefore only partially exploited: the British were given time to draw naval and air reinforcements to the Mediterranean to such an extent that a few months later the situation was again reversed, to our disadvantage; it continued to deteriorate until the final collapse, of which the withdrawal from North Africa in May, 1943, was the obvious proof.

But how great the danger which threatened the enemy was, and how near we were, after the blow delivered at Alexandria, to achieving decisive victory, was indicated, more clearly than by anyone else, by the man who, being in charge of the conduct of the war on the other side, realized it most fully: Winston Churchill. In a speech before a secret session of the House of Commons on April 23, 1942, after announcing the loss of the *Ark Royal*, the *Barham*, the *Repulse*, and the *Prince of Wales*, he continued as follows:

"A further sinister stroke was to come. On the early morning of December 19 half a dozen Italians in unusual diving suits were captured floundering about in the harbour of Alexandria. Extreme precautions have been taken for some time past against the varieties of human torpedo or one-man submarine entering our harbours. Not only are nets and other obstructions used but underwater charges are exploded at frequent irregular intervals in the fairway. None the less these men had penetrated the harbour. Four hours later explosions occurred in the bottoms of the *Valiant* and the *Queen Elizabeth*, produced by limpet bombs fixed with extraordinary courage and ingenuity, the effect of which was to blow large holes in the bottoms of both ships and to flood several compartments, thus putting them both out of action for many months. One ship will soon be ready again, the other is still in the floating dock at Alexandria, a constant target for enemy air attack. Thus we no longer had any battle squadron in the Mediterranean. *Barham* had gone and now *Valiant* and *Queen Elizabeth* were completely out of action. Both these ships floated on an even keel, they looked all right from the air. The enemy were for some time unaware of the success of their attack,[1] and it is only now that I feel it possible to make this disclosure to the House even in the strictness of a Secret Session. The Italian fleet still contains four or five battleships, several times repaired, of the new *Littorio* or of the modernized class. The sea defence of the Nile valley had to be confided to our submarine and destroyer flotillas, with a few cruisers, and of course to shore based Air forces. For this reason it was necessary to transfer a part of our shore based torpedo-carrying aircraft from the south and east coasts of England, where they were soon to be needed, to the north African shore . . ."

The decoration, that of the Military Order of Savoy, which was conferred upon me, on the king's own initiative, after the Alexandria operations, was accompanied by the following citation:

"Commanding officer of a submarine detailed to the Tenth Light Flotilla for special assault craft operations, he had already successfully carried out three daring and difficult undertakings; he studied and prepared, with great technical competence and shrewdness, the plan of a fourth operation, for forcing a further enemy base. He took his submarine close in to the heavily fortified harbor, facing with cool determination the risks incurred from the defense measures and vigilance of the enemy, in order to put the assault craft in the best possible position for forcing the enemy base. He then launched the assault craft in an action which achieved a brilliant success, leading as it did to the infliction of serious damage upon two enemy battleships."

[1] This assertion is disproved by the Italian war Bulletins quoted above. (Author's note.)

Comdr. Sam Dealey headed one of the submarine force's greatest fighting teams in the USS Harder. For five patrols Harder plagued the Japanese, only to be lost on her sixth patrol. Sam Dealey was awarded the Congressional Medal of Honor posthumously.

Hit 'em Again, *Harder*

WILLIAM C. CHANDLISS

By the late spring of 1944, American strategy in the Pacific was obvious to the Japanese. But that knowledge gave them little help, for their problem was to deploy their diminishing naval forces at the right time to the right place in an effort to blunt the head of each new American thrust. Such precise deployment required more than a knowledge of general strategy—it demanded that the Japanese high command know within very narrow limits of time just where the shifting, mobile carrier-borne lightning of the United States Pacific Fleet was going to strike next in paving the way for the amphibious assaults of the Marines that were whittling away the outlying holdings of the Empire of the Rising Sun.

Scheduled for mid-June was "Operation Forager," an invasion of the Japanese-held Mariana Islands. The capture of the Marianas would provide a base from which Air Corps bombers could strike at the Japanese home islands, something they had not been able to do since the beginning of the war except for the Halsey-Doolittle raid on Tokyo with bombers launched from the deck of the aircraft carrier Hornet some 600 miles off the Japanese coast on April 16, 1942.

To oppose the American seaborne invasion force, the Japanese high command devised the "A Go Plan," which called for simultaneous strikes by the Mobile Fleet, temporarily based at Tawitawi in the Philippines, and land-based planes from the Bonin Islands. To effect that kind of coordinated assault from two places so widely separated required perfect timing. If either element arrived ahead of the other it would face the terrible striking power of the United States Fifth Fleet aircraft carriers, battleships, and cruisers. So the

135

Japanese had to figure out where the American assault would take place and then so arrange matters that the Mobile Fleet departed Tawitawi at just the right time to be able to launch its carrier planes from the Philippine Sea to join with the land-based aircraft flying down from the Bonins.

In advance of setting "Forager" in motion, Admiral Nimitz, supreme commander in the Pacific, stationed submarines to watch the Mobile Fleet at Tawitawi and to patrol along its most probable routes to the scene of action.

When the first American carrier air strikes were launched against the Marianas, the enemy high command had to postpone its decision. Well aware of the speed and mobility of sea forces, the Tokyo headquarters knew that the strikes might be just a feint to draw them away from another likely invasion target, the Palau Islands farther to the south. When Tokyo finally decided that the Marianas, and particularly the island of Saipan, was the actual objective of the Nimitz campaign the signal was sent to put "A Go" into motion.

Unfortunately for the Japanese, their Mobile Fleet had fled from its anchorage at Tawitawi ahead of time and in consequence milled around aimlessly in the Philippine Sea waiting the word from Tokyo that would send the land-based planes winging southward from the Bonins. During that period of purposeless milling around, the Mobile Fleet was spotted by our submarines and the information thus provided enabled all other submarines to concentrate along its trail and warned the Fast Carrier Task Force under Admiral Mitscher to line up for an air strike. The result was the Battle of the Philippine Sea in which the Japanese lost two carriers to submarine attack and the astounding total of 476 planes in two days of air combat.

The historic, fatal mistiming of the Mobile Fleet's sortie from Tawitawi was the result of the work of a single submarine, Harder, whose assigned mission in that area was just to keep a watch on the Mobile Fleet and report what it was doing. But Comdr. Sam Dealey was not temperamentally suited to the passive role of an observer. As a result of Harder's operations around Tawitawi, the Mobile Fleet's veteran commander, Admiral Ozawa, decided that the area was so densely populated with American submarines that he dared not keep his ships there to wait for "A Go" to start.

IT WAS too dark to see him, but the bridge watch knew that Sam Dealey's full, smooth face was unruffled by any sign of concern. He never seemed to worry about anything. Just calmly surveyed whatever the situation might be, sometimes going so far as to squint his left eye slightly if something really critical developed.

At the moment there was nothing much to worry about. *Harder* was standing northward along the west coast of the Celebes, maneuvering to avoid collision with a host of fishing boats operating without navigation lights beneath an overcast sky in the Makassar Strait. Of course, any one of those fishing boats could be radio-equipped and might at the moment be sending an emergency signal for Japanese patrol boats to come out and sink *Harder*. But that was nothing new. *Harder* had been a target for enemy patrol boats many times. Commander Dealey would handle it, the crew knew, so they sailed on in the same carefree confidence that their skipper habitually displayed.

"Those British lads are still waiting near Dent Haven," said Lt. Comdr. Frank Lynch, *Harder's* executive officer. "We just picked a message off the Fox schedule saying that the other two boats had been unable to take them aboard."

"We'll try our best," Dealey rejoined. "After being in the Borneo jungle for two years reporting on the Japs they deserve to get out."

"Too bad they couldn't have walked south during those years," said Lynch. "I'd just as soon we didn't have to go through Sibutu Passage right now."

"Not getting nervous about the navigation, are you, Frank?" Dealey twitted.

"No more than usual in this part of the ocean. I'm about ready to trade in those charts for a good, reliable prayer book. Every time we take a sounding we turn up something that doesn't match the chart. We could find a nice surprise right near the surface almost anytime."

"Could be. I'm keeping her trimmed deep around here so we'll have a couple of feet to gain by blowing if we do go aground."

"That'll help some," Lynch admitted, "provided we don't get ourselves impaled on a pinnacle. That wreck we passed yesterday near Cape William was piled up where the chart shows ten fathoms. He hit something real sharp and real sudden."

Dealey called down the conning-tower hatch for a sharp course change to avoid a fishing boat looming up in the darkened sea.

"A bit of moonlight would be a help right now," he muttered.

"That'll come when we meet our first Japanese patrol boat," said Lynch. "It will light us up nice and clear for his deck gun."

"Well, we're not looking for trouble this time," Dealey reminded him. "Our job is to get up to North Borneo and take out those Britishers, and then have a quiet look at Tawitawi. We're not trying to stir up anything."

"Oh sure," Lynch answered ironically. "And if we should see an enemy destroyer we'll just duck out of the way until he goes by."

"Well, that depends. We will if we can. Of course, if it looks like it would delay us too long to go around him I guess we'd just have to sink him. But we're not going to look for trouble."

"We've never had to," said Lynch. "Enough of it comes looking for us to keep the tracking party from getting out of practice."

Dealey pounded the bridge rail in irritation as another dark shape hove in sight close aboard.

"I'd ram if I were sure we wouldn't damage the stem," he growled.

"You couldn't do that," Lynch observed. "That might come under the heading of looking for trouble. We're a real peaceful ship on this trip."

Half an hour of broken-field running carried *Harder* clear of the fishing fleet. The radarscope showed clear except for the high hills on Borneo's east coast. With course shaped to pass Tandjoeng Mangkalihat 4 miles on the port hand, Dealey turned over the con to Lynch and went below. Although there was a normal watch bill in effect which included all qualified officers on the ship, it was an unwritten rule that Dealey, Lynch, or Sam Logan, the torpedo officer, would be on the bridge when in doubtful waters. In June, 1944, the Makassar Strait qualified as doubtful water.

Shortly before dawn, Dealey relieved Lynch at the con and took *Harder* below for the usual precautionary dive at the approach of daylight. Under a heavy overcast the shoreline of Mangkalihat lay broad on the port beam. *Harder* stood onward into the Celebes Sea for another hour, then hauled to the northwest to pass between Batu and Maratua en route to Tarakan Island. Occasional radar bearings showed that they were barely creeping against the southerly set of the current. Dealey begrudged the loss of time that the need for submergence was costing them.

"This is sort of going the long way around to Sibutu, isn't it?"

Lynch asked. "Couldn't be that you figure on falling in with a Japanese convoy coming out of Tarakan."

"It adds only 20 miles," Dealey told him. "And we might just as well pick up some information on ship movements around Tarakan while we're going this way."

The voice of the talker cut in on them.

"Sonar reports rainsquall ahead."

Dealey motioned up the periscope. A monsoon thunderstorm sending down sheets of rain cut off vision half a mile ahead. In the intervening clear area nothing was to be seen.

"Surface," Dealey ordered.

Harder planed up, and Dealey and the lookouts raced to the bridge when she broke clear. With all diesels on the line at standard speed, they plowed into the rain. Visibility dropped to 300 yards.

"Sail on the starboard bow!" a lookout yelled.

A two-masted schooner, scudding along under shortened sail, stood across their track.

"Come right to three five zero," Dealey sang out. "All ahead full."

The schooner had a radio antenna strung between her fore and main masts. She dropped out of sight in the slicing rain as *Harder* swept past under her stern.

"That guy will have the airfield at Tarakan filled in on our position right pronto," Lynch said.

"It won't do them any good," Dealey commented. "Their planes couldn't find us in this stuff."

An hour later, still plowing through the squall at full speed, they heard distant depth-charging far astern on the bearing of their contact with the sailing vessel. The schooner had obviously made a contact report that brought surface patrol boats to the scene. Reassured that their position was not being accurately plotted by the enemy, Dealey reduced *Harder* to standard speed and continued on toward Tarakan. Under clearing skies at sunset he stood past the island hopefully at slow speed, but no inviting targets hove in sight. He changed course to the northeast for the entrance to Sibutu Passage, following the convoy route between Tarakan and the Philippines.

At dawn, *Harder* was 30 miles southeast of the passage. The transit of Sibutu is a tricky business at best, with strong, variable currents making it almost impossible to execute at the slow sub-

139

merged speed of a fleet submarine. At the moment it presented additional hazards in the presence of the Japanese Mobile Fleet at Tawitawi on the eastern side of the passage. A surface transit at high speed was their only choice, and that meant going through at night in the hope of avoiding detection by the enemy surface patrol in the 17-mile bottleneck through which they must pass.

Dealey took *Harder* down to 250 feet to loaf through the daylight hours and give the crew a rest for the busy, taut times that lay ahead. Assuming no untoward event during their run through Sibutu Passage, they still faced a complex problem in running close to the enemy-held Borneo shore and getting the waiting British agents aboard without being detected.

As they crept along with just enough speed to give effect to the diving planes, Dealey and Lynch reviewed their plans to snatch the British intelligence agents off Borneo and make their getaway. Back at their base at Fremantle, Australia, the whole thing had been rehearsed in the usual thorough Dealey manner, with every contingency they could think of cranked into the problem. But Sam Dealey was a perfectionist who never assumed that anything was foolproof, which was one of the reasons why *Harder* had piled up a distinguished combat record under his command.

Half an hour before sunset they came to periscope depth. The sky was mostly clear, with occasional cumulus clouds of fair weather drifting lazily across the Celebes Sea. The bright light of the setting sun etched Sibutu Peak and Bongao Island clearly against the blue sky. Sibutu bore 340° and Bongao 006°. They hauled to the northwest and went ahead at one-third speed, ready to surface for the high-speed transit after sundown.

"That moonlight you were wishing for farther south will be with us," Lynch said. "It will be a big help—to the enemy patrol."

"We'll keep to the Sibutu Island side and try to stay in the shadow as much as we can," Dealey decided. "With luck we can have our passengers aboard with a couple of hours of darkness to spare."

"Moonset tonight will be about three hours before dawn," Lynch told him. "So we'll be in real dark while we're doing the job."

Impatiently, Dealey ordered the periscope up for a look to check the progress he knew could not be better than about three knots. The two high islands so clearly visible only ten minutes earlier were entirely blotted out by a sudden squall.

"Surface!" he ordered happily.

At full speed, *Harder* planed up, shifted to diesel drive, and bored into the storm at a satisfying 19 knots. At times, in the densest periods of the storm, radar could see as little as the straining eyes of the bridge lookouts, but with the wide stretch of water that was Sibutu Passage, Dealey plunged *Harder* confidently on her way, her position intermittently confirmed by sketchy radar bearings on the landmarks.

"Contact bearing three five five, range two oh oh double oh!"

"Battle stations, torpedo!" Dealey responded automatically.

For a few minutes nothing further came from the radar operator. But Dealey noted with satisfaction that during those few minutes the faint sky light which had trickled through the rain barrier disappeared. The sun had set.

"Contact now bears three five zero, range one eight oh double oh!"

Without waiting for the tracking party's report, Dealey readily saw that *Harder* was in an ideal position for an approach to whatever lay out there in the storm. The target's change in bearing and range showed that it was heading southward and that *Harder* was off on the port bow.

"Target group five ships," radar amplified.

"Target speed fourteen, course one seven five," Lynch added from his plotting board.

"Flank speed," Dealey responded. "Come left to two seven zero."

The new course and speed would assure that *Harder* kept ahead of the approaching ships and close enough to their track for a final submerged approach.

"Target in sight, sir!" the forward lookout shouted. "Three tankers and two destroyers."

A report like that in almost total darkness and with diminishing but still appreciable rain would ordinarily be greeted with skepticism. But Sam Dealey knew his men, knew the endless hours of drill that had trained them to a fine pitch in all phases of detection and attack. He swung his own glasses on the reported bearing and confirmed without surprise that the lookout's report was exactly right. The three tankers were in line, with the destroyers out as flankers on either bow of the leading ship.

Suddenly the rain stopped. The near destroyer showed up clearly silhouetted against a background of moonlight through a break in the racing clouds. The range was 8 miles.

"Clear the bridge," Dealey told his lookouts.

The patch of moonlight that had illuminated the convoy was racing toward *Harder* as the broken cumulo-nimbus clouds swept along on a 30-knot wind. To submerge would probably hide *Harder* from detection, but it would also mean a speed loss that could let the convoy get beyond convenient attack position. Dealey wanted none of that. He held on at maximum speed with the range growing shorter by the minute.

And then it happened. The light of the brilliant moon flooded over *Harder* and brought prompt evidence that the Japanese lookouts were on the job. The near destroyer swept around in a high-speed turn, pouring a cloud of smoke to shield the tankers, and stood directly for the approaching submarine.

"Come left to one five zero!" Dealey shouted down the conning-tower hatch. He figured that the destroyer might decide not to get too far from the tankers for fear of exposing them to attack from another submarine. But the Japanese skipper promptly demonstrated that he was more anxious to sink *Harder* than he was to fend off a submarine that wasn't there. With her diesels putting out everything they had, *Harder* left a broad white wake streaming astern and the destroyer knifed along through that trail of foam, closing the range with a speed advantage of a good ten knots.

In leisurely fashion Dealey descended the ladder to the conning tower and dogged the hatch behind him. Ordering up the scope, he trained it astern on their pursuer. With that surface killer still 6 miles astern, there was a chance that a quick dive to deep water coupled with a quick turn and a shift to silent running would hide them long enough to force him to give up the chase in order not to lose his convoy. But Sam Dealey had other plans.

"We'll let him gain until he starts shooting," he explained to Lynch. "Then we'll see what can be done about him."

The long chase gave him plenty of time to figure the destroyer's speed accurately at 26 knots. There was no doubt about his course because it was right down *Harder*'s wake.

"Range nine oh double oh," radar reported. It checked with the stadimeter in the periscope.

"This guy must be planning to board us," Dealey grinned happily.

At the TDC, Sam Logan cranked in range and bearing data, maintaining a continuous setup for the time when Dealey should decide to attack. Their thorough drilling, both in practice and in combat, had welded Dealey and his tracking party into a unit which acted with the speed and precision of a football team when he called the signals.

"He's a dope not to use his forward guns," Dealey commented casually. "He's just getting himself into a lot of trouble."

Letting a destroyer chase him on the surface to within a few thousand yards would move some people to think that Sam Dealey was letting *Harder* in for trouble. But that kind of thinking on the part of enemy skippers had resulted in their finding themselves fresh out of ships.

"Range seven five double oh," radar reported.

"That's close enough for our purposes," Dealey observed. "Take her down to 60 feet. All ahead one-third. Come left to zero nine zero."

The submarine slid under smoothly, shifting easily to electric drive, and steadied exactly on course and at depth in a matter of seconds.

"Set torpedoes for 6 feet," Dealey directed in the casual manner of a man telling a waiter how he wanted his steak prepared.

On the surface the destroyer raced along on a set course down the wake. Dealey could picture the captain and lookouts trying to spot the submarine that suddenly wasn't there anymore.

"Angle on the bow port 30. . . . Range, mark! . . . Bearing, mark!"

"Set," Logan answered promptly.

"Fire one . . . fire two . . . fire three."

The dead silence that always follows the firing of torpedoes settled over the conning tower and control room. Logan studied the sweep of his stopwatch hand, counting off the calculated running time to the target. Dealey, observing through the periscope, could see the wake of one of the missiles foaming on the moonlit sea. Possibly the destroyer captain saw it, too. But at a range now down to 1,150 yards there was nothing he could do about it.

"Number one missed," Logan observed as the watch passed the calculated time of impact. Dealey shrugged slightly. It really was not too important.

143

There was no need for Logan to report on number two and number three. Dealey saw a towering sheet of flame light up the sea for miles around them, its bright light flashing into his face from the periscope eyepiece. A few seconds later everyone in *Harder* felt the twin shock of the explosions and the secondary rumble of ammunition and fuel exploding in the target's hull.

"Surface," Dealey broke the conversational void. "Fire control party to the bridge."

When he and the others got topside, the stern of the destroyer had risen to a vertical angle. Around the plunging wreck great spouts of water shot upward as the ready depth charges, intended for *Harder*, helped crush their own ship.

"Nice work, boys," Sam told the firing group. It was characteristic of him that he invited them up to see the triumph of their calculations. Mostly, it was only the skipper and the lookouts who got a view of what had been accomplished in a submerged attack.

In the comparative darkness that fell when the destroyer took her final plunge, the flickering light of a Franklin-type life buoy bobbed in the swirl of waves radiating from the point where she had slipped below. Dealey maneuvered slowly toward it, warning the lookouts to keep an eye peeled for survivors. There was no one hanging to the buoy. There was no one anywhere.

"All ahead full," Dealey called out. "Come left to two four zero."

Harder was off in pursuit of the fleeing convoy now short one destroyer in its escort.

"Just thought I'd mention that Dent Haven is over that way," Lynch remarked gently, pointing beyond the starboard quarter.

"It will stay there, I'm sure," Dealey answered with a grin. "Right now I want to try out my theory that we can overhaul that convoy before it reaches Tarakan."

Just short of an hour later radar picked up another target dead ahead. The range was closing at something like 40 knots. It meant only one thing: the other destroyer was headed their way and bent on serious business.

"Clear the bridge! Dive! Dive!"

Dealey kept the periscope cross hairs on the charging destroyer while Lynch called off the range and bearing data to the tracking party. At just over 1,000 yards *Harder* let go a spread of six torpedoes. The destroyer wove like a ball carrier in a broken field and

144

Dealey quickly saw that the enemy skipper's superb ship handling was going to keep him clear of the missiles.

"Three hundred feet," Dealey shouted. "Rig for depth charge. Silent running."

Harder took a normal down angle and raced for the depth. As the depth gauge neared the 300-foot mark the ship suddenly pushed over to 15 degrees and plunged downward past her safety mark. They could hear the creak of her hull plates being squeezed by increasing pressure.

"All hands aft!" Dealey shouted.

Crewmen thrown from their feet by the unexpected tilt climbed upright and raced toward the stern to right the ship. Abruptly, *Harder* took an upward slant and started for the surface as the first five depth charges tore at her hull. Water spouted from the antenna trunk and splashed onto the deck. Amid the roar and shock of the barrage Dealey coached the men forward until the ship was once more on an even keel. The depth-charging ceased as the destroyer finished his run and rounded to for a new pass at them.

"Everything's under control now," Lynch reported.

"What went wrong?" Dealey demanded.

"We had one of the new men on the stern planes," Lynch told him. "He didn't remember that the indicator light goes off when we rig for silent running. So he thought he'd lost power and shifted to hand operation. Then he gave her a twist in the wrong direction and things began to happen."

Dealey nodded. *Harder* had taken aboard twenty replacements just before shoving off on her current patrol.

"I guess all the drills in the world don't prove a thing until a man's operated under battle conditions."

"High-speed propellers approaching!"

The report from sonar reminded them that the surface enemy was coming in for a renewed attack. They heard the ominous explosions clearly, but it was obvious that the destroyer had lost good sound contact thanks to the reflective quality of thermal layers in the depths where they hid. After twenty minutes of futile depth-charging, the destroyer shoved off to rejoin his convoy.

Shortly after midnight *Harder* surfaced.

"Any idea where we are?" Dealey asked.

"Not very precisely," Lynch admitted. "This damned haze makes

145

it impossible to get a decent sight. We've plotted a moon line and two stars, but the lines form a pretty large triangle on the chart. The best 'guesstimate' is that we're 85 miles bearing one eighty-seven from Sibutu lighthouse."

"And those disobliging Japanese won't turn the light on for us," Dealey said. "So we'll just take it easy on course zero one zero until daylight and then see what we can pick up. Put two engines on charge and make turns for 10 knots."

Heavy haze approaching the density of fog enveloped the Celebes Sea. With nothing to look at it was impossible to estimate visibility. Neither radar nor sonar picked up anything interesting as *Harder* stood northward through the night. The fathometer reassuringly registered safe water underfoot. The hours of darkness crept by quietly. At five-thirty, with sunrise half an hour away, Dealey took her to periscope depth.

Dawn, such as it was, arrived on time, disclosing a hazy stretch of empty sea beneath the heavy overcast of a stationary front. Rain showers, triggered off in the unstable air, dotted the horizon in all quadrants. *Harder* eased along at an economical one-third speed on a heading designed to bring her off the entrance to Sibutu at noon. Disappointed at being late for his rendezvous with the secret agents ashore, Dealey planned a daylight transit of the passage if weather offered a reasonable cover.

"Mast bearing zero zero five."

The report from the periscope watch brought Dealey to the conning tower. Faintly visible through a light rain shower, a single spar reared above the horizon. Dealey sent *Harder* down to 80 feet for a concealed approach. Ten minutes later he ordered her up for another periscope look. She had just begun to climb when the hull shook in violent collision and the bow took an abrupt upward tilt that forced her crew to grab hold of whatever was near to keep on their feet.

"All back full," Dealey ordered. "Blow main ballast."

Harder broached with 2 knots of sternway. In the slightly better light, Dealey could see a tall, virtually limbless tree rising from a low island about 5 miles away—the "mast" on which they had been making their attack approach. Close to the bow, tidal ripples told the story of their collision. They had scraped a submerged reef.

"Apparently we were set to the southwest during the night," Dealey wrote in the log. "Fortunately we suffered no damage as a result of the grounding, and were able to identify the island and its tree so as to fix our position."

Screened by squalls, *Harder* proceeded on the surface on course zero three zero to pass through deep water and line up the southern approach to Sibutu Passage. At midmorning, radar contact on a rapidly approaching airplane sent them diving to 100 feet. They sweated out the minutes of waiting for an aerial depth-charging, and when nothing happened concluded that their evasive dive had been successful.

"High-speed propellers bearing zero two five!"

The sonar report bespoke the fact that the aircraft had indeed spotted them and called on the surface forces for the kill. Already submerged below periscope depth, *Harder* could easily go deep to avoid detection.

"Take her up to 60 feet," was Sam Dealey's solution.

As the periscope broke the surface, Dealey got an intimate portrait of a *Fubuki*-class destroyer just under 4,000 yards away and bearing down in a manner that left no doubt he had excellent information on their position. The charging menace was being expertly handled, coming at them in a series of constant helm course changes that made a successful torpedo setup impossible at normal ranges. Sam Dealey found a ready solution for that one. Let the destroyer come in so close that it would be almost impossible for the torpedoes to miss. The corollary that it would be quite impossible for the destroyer to miss if the torpedo spread should go wrong was, in Dealey's way of thinking, quite beside the point.

"Range . . . mark!"

"One oh double oh," Lynch read off.

Logan waited expectantly for the order to fire. He had already set up the torpedoes for shallow run and a one-quarter degree spread.

"Range . . . mark!"

"Seven double oh."

The low rumble of the destroyer's propellers was plainly audible throughout the hull."

"Range . . . mark!"

"Six five oh!"

The destroyer's superstructure completely filled the periscope eyepiece.

"Fire one . . . two . . . three!"

Dealey's count sent the torpedoes away at three-second intervals, just far enough apart to keep them from interfering with each other.

"All ahead full. Full right rudder."

In the midst of their frantic turn to avoid collision head on with the slashing bow now only a little more than 500 feet away, *Harder* was slammed far over to starboard by a monstrous push as though a giant creature of the deep had seized her periscope and was turning her over. It was a deafeningly noisy creature, too, as noisy as a destroyer being rent into a thousand pieces by the explosion of her ammunition, her boilers, and one well-placed enemy torpedo.

Harder righted herself slowly.

"Steady on one eight five." Dealey spoke without taking his eyes from the periscope.

"Okay, my friends," he called below to the tracking party. "Come on up and take a look at your handiwork. Better make it fast so you get here while there's still something to see."

There was something to see for a few more minutes. The torn mess of twisted steel that a few minutes before had been a *Fubuki*-class destroyer now poised ridiculously with its bow in the air, but with nothing to be seen of its stern, if indeed it still had one.

"High-speed propellers bearing two seven zero!"

Dealey swung the periscope to port in time to see a sister of the doomed ship driving toward them. For a bare instant he hesitated, weighing the chances of taking on the newcomer with only three torpedoes left in the bow tubes. The same number had been adequate for their recent victim, and might suffice this time.

"Take her to two sixty," he ordered with a hint of regret in his voice. The time remaining to make a setup coupled with partially loaded tubes would give the avenging destroyer more advantage than he needed.

Dealey watched the dial on the conning tower registering the change in water temperature. As they passed the 200-foot mark he saw it wiggle perceptibly. *Harder* had passed a thermal layer which would bounce back the pinging of the surface hunter's sound gear.

"Come right to three five zero," Dealey conned. "Rig for silent running."

Some distance astern, near enough to be heard but far enough to be safe, a vengeful, high-density depth-charge attack churned the water near the grave of the sunken destroyer. Her surviving sister was doing its best. Fortunately for *Harder*, it was not quite good enough. The submarine crept quietly away.

"Secure from battle stations," Dealey spoke over the intercom. "Take a rest until the next destroyer comes asking for it."

It was a little past noon. For five hours *Harder* and her men had stalked and been stalked, had gone through a grounding that could have ended with them all in the hands of an enemy notoriously brutal in his treatment of prisoners of war. The reef-studded boundaries of Sibutu Strait were shrinking in on these brash men who persisted in stirring things up only 20 miles from the main anchorage of the Combined Fleet. Dealey knew that stark military necessity would compel Admiral Ozawa to dispose of this menace lying on the patch of his fleet's sortie route. It was time for *Harder* to get out of there, to enjoy the plaudits her triumphs had earned.

For three hours Dealey kept her down. It could have been called a rest period. But it was a period of rest beset by anxieties which would try the souls of ordinary men. Through their listening gear came the sound of ever increasing pinging from bearings all around the compass, grim evidence that Admiral Ozawa had sent out destroyers in force with orders to rid his fleet of this hidden threat. And as they drifted along in the gloomy depths of Sibutu Passage, they knew that at any moment the vagaries of current might impale them on a reef from which, if they were fortunate, they might escape by coming up and exposing themselves to the desperate hunters on the surface.

For Dealey it was a heavy burden of decision. There was still a good store of power in the batteries. Their position was fairly well fixed during the battle with the destroyer. A straight run south at one-third speed would almost certainly carry them clear of the tightening patrol noose into the wide reaches of the Celebes Sea. If their luck held, they could evade detection until nightfall and make a fast surface run out of trouble.

"Explosions on bearing two four zero," sonar reported. "Sounds like aircraft dropping charges."

The escape gap was narrowing. If enough planes and destroyers got into the act it would just be a matter of time. Dealey studied

149

the faces of the men in the conning tower. The youngster at the helm was one of the new men who had joined them at Fremantle. He stared stolidly at the gyro compass. Dealey glanced at his hands and noted that they held the wheel firmly but not tensely, that the movement of the wheel was smooth and gentle with none of the overcorrection that signals nervous tension. He'd do.

Dealey lowered himself down the ladder to the control room. The bow planesman, a *Harder* veteran, eased the wheel with his left hand while he tapped the ashes from his cigarette with his right. Casual but alert, his eyes never left the bubble of the inclinometer. Beside him, at the stern plane control, Dealey recognized the youngster whose jumpiness had so nearly brought them to grief during the first destroyer battle. He silently commended Frank Lynch's good judgment in seeing to it that the kid had been kept on the diving party watch list. Everybody makes a mistake. The test is how well a man learns from an error. Dealey crossed to the stern planesman's station.

"You're holding a good steady bubble, son," he said.

The youngster's face flushed with pleasure.

"Thank you, sir." He hesitated a moment. "That bust won't happen again, Captain." He was remembering the past, and he knew that it was not being held against him.

The bow planesman looked up at Sam Dealey and winked the approval of an old shipmate. He understood the Dealey theory of leadership, to know and be known to every man in the crew, to make them understand that to him they were people, important people. That was what made *Harder* the ship she was.

Near the TDC, Sam Logan and two enlisted men chatted casually over cups of coffee, an occasional laugh revealing that they were engaged in the sailor's favorite relaxation pastime of telling stories that gained in humor what they might lose in accuracy with the passage of time.

The men of *Harder* were taking it easy. What mattered it to them that a couple of hundred feet above a desperate enemy was cunningly and determinedly working toward their destruction? Sam Dealey would lead them along the right course.

He rejoined Lynch in the conning tower.

"About time we took another look," he said. "Bring her up to periscope depth."

Sibutu Strait sparkled in the bright afternoon sun. The northern semicircle of the horizon was clear. But the swinging periscope picked up two destroyers 5 miles to southward, steering a zigzag pattern, line abreast 1,000 yards apart. Their bow wave pattern told Dealey that their speed was around 14 knots, fast enough to cover a lot of ground without reducing the effectiveness of their probing sonar.

"Battle stations, torpedo," Dealey spoke. "Come right to one eight five. Bow tubes ready."

To save the battery, to keep down propeller noise, and to take advantage of the fact that the enemy was headed their way, Dealey held *Harder* at one-third speed. In a series of quick looks with the periscope, he plotted the timing and course change of the enemy zigzag plan, and maneuvered *Harder* with small course changes that would bring her into attack position. The distance dropped to 2 miles with no sign of alarm on the part of the two ships. Then a string of flags raced up the halyards of the one on the right, promptly repeated by her consort. Dealey tensed, for the bunting could be the signal for an attack. The flags came down in the traditional sign to execute whatever maneuver was called for. In precise synchronism, the bows swung toward *Harder*. But the unseen helmsmen did not check on an attack heading. The ships continued through their arc and finally settled down on a reverse course away from *Harder*. They were clearly assigned to sweep the southern area of the passage.

"Secure from battle stations," Dealey ordered.

"We'll hold on this heading," he added to Lynch, "and be ready for them when they start back."

Lynch acknowledged the decision without surprise. To many an able submariner, the appearance of one destroyer, even one not clearly on the alert for trouble in the vicinity, was considered ample reason for going somewhere else in search of easier game. That Sam Dealey would deliberately plan an attack on two of them who were out to get his ship in the entrapment of confined waters was just as much to be expected as was the alternative course by other captains.

With the periscope housed to avoid a revealing feather, *Harder* plodded along on the trail of the retiring enemy. A quick look every five minutes disclosed that they were still headed toward the southern end of the strait. Then something new was added. Eyeing his quarry, Dealey picked up the distant flash of a signal searchlight far down on the southern horizon. He saw a signalman on one of his targets shuttering an answer. The meaning of the exchange became evident on the next periscope sweep with the appearance of the foremasts of four new destroyers standing northward to join their friends.

"They're putting six on the line," he told Lynch when the periscope had been sent down. "That means one for each of our bow torpedoes. I think the odds are getting a little bit too long."

"I'm inclined to agree," Lynch replied fervently. "We ought to make it a policy not to take on more than two or three at a time."

"An excellent thought." Dealey smiled. "Let's get going out of here and pick up our passengers."

Harder came around to a northerly course and crept along at 100 feet until the conning-tower clock told them the sun was setting. Dealey brought her to periscope depth. The six destroyers, sailing abreast, were combing the passage some 10 miles astern. In the half-hour of remaining daylight they would make good on their zig-zag course enough distance to close the range to a little under 6 miles. It would be touch and go when they came to the surface.

"Keep a radar watch ahead when we come up," Dealey directed. "But don't train it aft. There's no use getting those tin cans all excited at this point."

Under a cloudless sky with a bright moon just above the horizon, *Harder* came to the surface. With two engines on the job of charging her dangerously depleted battery, she was able to keep the distance from the destroyers constant on the propulsion power of her number three and four diesels. Dealey had reason to be thankful that Sibutu Passage extended north and south, for on that line of bearing *Harder* would not be silhouetted against the moon for the benefit of her pursuers. His own lookouts, knowing where the destroyers were, had no difficulty picking up their shadowy outlines against the southern sky.

"Contact! Small object dead ahead, range one five double oh!"

All hands tensed at the report from radar plot. A small object could mean any of a lot of things, none of them good.

"Right full rudder," Dealey told the helmsman.

The bearing of the small target, now visible from the bridge, swung satisfyingly to the left. Whatever it might be, it was not as yet pursuing *Harder*. A few minutes later, close aboard on the port beam, they made out a spiny pinnacle of rock past which tide-driven water swirled ominously.

"Well," Lynch remarked philosophically, "there's one more to report to the Hydrographic Office. Wonder if we get any extra credit for finding rocks and shoals that don't appear on the charts."

"Credit for missing them is good enough for me," Dealey retorted. "Pass the word to the radar operator that I thank him for a good job."

At three in the morning, they cleared the northern mouth of Sibutu Passage and came to heading 280° for the run to the rendezvous on the Borneo coast. A brief radio message to Commander, Submarines, Seventh Fleet, advised that *Harder* would be ready for the intelligence agents shortly after sunset the following night. Dealey wanted a full day to study the navigational hazards with which he would have to deal when his submarine nosed close to the treacherous shore where reefs and possibly an enemy ambush lay in wait for them.

At sunrise *Harder* submerged with Mount Hattan's 2,000-foot peak just showing above the horizon. Slowly the lower portions of the northeast Borneo Peninsula lifted into view, and by midafternoon they were coasting 2 miles off the mangrove swamps fringing the entrance to Dent Haven. The penciled sketch which was to guide them to the point of embarkation showed a low sandy beach south-southwestward of the harbor, backed by dense jungle. It was a fine guide for hikers, but lacked information on what lay beneath the surface offshore. Through the long day of waiting, Dealey took visual bearings on anything that could be identified as a landmark, and had the radar scan them so that the operator would recognize them after dark. By nightfall, that few miles of Borneo coast was probably the most thoroughly charted stretch of beach on earth.

In a calm sea and bright moonlight, Dealey brought *Harder* to the surface and gingerly started her shoreward. On the forward deck lay two rubber boats fitted with small outboard motors. Sticking upward from the motors were thin masts supporting an array of wires, special reflectors designed by *Harder*'s radar gang so that they would be able to keep track of the boats as they made their way to the beach.

"By the mark, six!"

The voice of a leadsman stationed near the bow floated aft in the quiet night, telling Dealey that there were 36 feet of water above the shelving bottom. *Harder* with her present load and trim was drawing 16 feet.

"By the deep, five!"

"All stop," Dealey spoke quietly. The diesel exhaust snuffed to inactivity. *Harder* glided forward by momentum in a sudden near silence, broken only by the lap of ripples against her rounded sides. Eyes and ears strained for anything on that lifeless shore that might be a sign of trouble. *Harder* was a sitting duck if their plan had leaked to the enemy.

"And a half, four!"

"All back one." Briefly the propellers spun, then halted at Dealey's next command. The submarine lay dead in the water. Without any spoken order from the bridge, the special detail forward lowered the two rubber boats over the side. Their small outboards stuttered to life, and they crept shoreward, one man in each.

At Dealey's side a radioman pressed the button of a walkie-talkie.

"Coach to team, testing."

The earpiece of his set rattled tinnily as the men in the boats came up on the circuit.

"Communications okay, sir," the radioman reported.

At best it would be nearly two hours before the return of the boats. Although the shore lay only 1,000 yards away, the slow speed of the awkward craft made it a long journey. Then, too, there would have to be an exchange of prearranged signals before the visitors and their future passengers were satisfied that each was really friendly and not the bait in a clever trap. The enemy had shown himself able to adapt to jungle operations and to practice deception that could cost the unwary their lives. On the bridge, Dealey grinned as he saw men surreptitiously checking their watches while the boats were still in sight.

Ten minutes after shoving off, the boats were lost to sight. The sound grew faint in the distance.

"Radar reports the boats are off course to the left," the bridge talker told Dealey. "They're heading for a reef."

Dealey took the walkie-talkie from his radioman.

"Team, this is coach. Steer 15 degrees to the right of your present course."

"One, wilco. . . . Two, wilco," came the response.

In a few minutes, the radar operator reported they were back on the track, and Dealey gave them a new heading to keep them that way. Once more the bridge grew quiet. Twenty minutes. Forty minutes. Fifty-five minutes.

"Coach, this is One. Recognition signals exchanged. We're going in."

The plan provided that one boat would go ashore first, while the other lay off ready to signal *Harder* if anything suspicious developed.

"Radar contact. Aircraft. Bearing one two zero. Range two oh oh double oh."

With a slant range of only 20,000 yards, the plane's intentions would soon be known. Dealey had to make his decision right away. If the plane were coming after them, his only hope would be to get out to deeper water. But to do that meant leaving the small boats behind and the strong probability that they could not be recovered before daylight, for the small radar reflectors would not show up much more than a few miles.

"Bearing constant. Range one six oh double oh."

"Flood her down!" Dealey shouted down the conning-tower hatch.

Air gushed through the main ballast tank vents, water rose over the main-deck superstructure. *Harder* settled lightly on the bottom with the water halfway up to the bridge. Dealey was gambling on the small protrusion of the bridge giving to the searching eyes of the enemy pilot the appearance of just another rock amid the reef-strewn waters of the coast.

The blue flame of the plane's exhaust showed up against the night sky. It held a constant course toward their position. In two minutes he would be at the release point for a string of bombs, if such was in his planning. The two minutes seemed like two hours. The plane droned on through the night, disappearing beyond the high hills on course toward the Asian mainland.

Somehow the fact the aircraft had paid them no heed seemed to engender the feeling that their mission was unsuspected by the enemy. The thought process was illogical, as each would readily have admitted, for a transport plane on a routine mission would not have been involved in an action against enemy coastal raiders. But spirits rose sharply among the men on the submarine's bridge sweating out the return of the boats.

"Coach, this is One. Passengers embarked. Both boats coming out."

It seemed only a fraction of the time taken for the shoreward trip when the two rubber boats emerged from the shadows into the moonlight bathing *Harder*. With the submarine's main deck still below water, the two rubber boats came alongside the ladder from the main deck to the bridge.

Six gaunt, bewhiskered men climbed wearily up the ladder, spoke their greeting and their gratitude to Dealey in English and Australian accents, and were gently hurried below. Every minute counted against the time left to work clear into the Sulu Sea. The boats were maneuvered into position above the main deck, and Dealey neatly brought the submarine up under them. In a trice, the boats were deflated and struck below.

"All back full!" Dealey called below. "Let's get out of here!"

Clear of the shoal area, *Harder* went all ahead full on four engines, swept round to course 102°, and headed for Sibutu Passage. Sam Dealey's orders had been to patrol the passage en route to Borneo and then, at discretion, to scout northeastward along the Sulu Archipelago to Zamboanga, transit the Basilan Strait, and return to Australia. There was plenty of fuel in the tanks, and there were several torpedoes in the tubes and in the torpedo-room racks. Dealey figured another look at Sibutu was indicated.

Dawn found them 20 miles north of Sibutu. So did a Japanese seaplane. In a crash descent that brought the weary Borneo passengers tumbling from their bunks to the roar of the diving alarm, *Harder* slanted for deep water. In the glassy sea, the enemy aviator had a fine view of the submarine's outline, a fact the *Harder* men realized when a single depth charge knocked out the main lighting circuit as they crossed the 100-foot mark. At 250 feet they found a negative thermocline, slowed to silent running, and stood to the northeast away from Sibutu. For the rest of the day *Harder* clung to that safe haven, the peace of mind of her crew and passengers marred only by the sound of destroyer screws passing directly overhead or close aboard. No depth charges came their way. The blessed thermal, mirroring the surface ships' sonar probes, shielded them from detection.

At sundown, Dealey brought her up. The battery needed charging and the air needed freshening. A moderate breeze blew from the northwest.

"Steer one eight five," he told the helmsman.

With the battery on charge, *Harder* once more headed for Sibutu. By eleven that night they were a scant 8 miles from the Mobile Fleet's anchorage at Tawitawi.

"Two ships dead ahead, sir!"

"Radar contact bearing one eight five, range eight oh double oh!"

Human and electronic eyes had picked up the enemy destroyers at the same instant. Through his night glasses, Dealey picked them out on a searching zigzag pattern that showed Admiral Ozawa was not relaxing the screening of his fleet's anchorage. Astern lay relative safety for *Harder*, as yet undetected by the hunters. Sam Dealey went ahead.

With clockwork precision, all hands manned their battle stations as *Harder* went to periscope depth 2 miles in the van of the enemy ships.

"Two sets of propeller noises," sonar reported. "Turn count 15 knots."

The setup was perfect for the leading destroyer, but Dealey waited. The two ships were due to change course in their zigzag pattern, and the new heading would put them both in the line of fire—unless, of course, they spotted *Harder* first and roared in for the attack. At a range of 1,200 yards they commenced to swing, just as Dealey had expected. At 800 yards they had settled down, the bow of the far destroyer just visible beyond the broadside of the nearer.

"Fire one . . . two . . . three . . . four!"

As the last torpedo left its tube, Dealey called for an emergency turn, for the range had shortened to the point where *Harder* would hit the target even if the torpedoes missed.

In rapid succession, three towering spouts rose skyward along the near destroyer's side, lit up like illuminated fountains by the detonation of her magazines. Guns, stacks, and bridge superstructure exploded through the glare of her death. Fifteen seconds later, the fourth torpedo ripped into the side of the far destroyer, which had not even had time to start an evasive turn.

Once more, Dealey brought *Harder* to the surface to survey the

157

results. Invited up with the fire control party was the senior member of the rescued group.

The first destroyer, broken into three pieces which drifted apart as they sank, went under in less than five minutes. Her partner, slowly heeling over, spouted from her flaming magazines ammunition that screamed across the night sky.

Turning from the panorama of destruction, Dealey saw his Australian passenger's face illuminated in the light from the dying ship. The man seemed hypnotized by the spectacle. His mouth broke into a smile when he noticed Dealey watching his reactions.

"I say, Captain," he remarked. "If you chaps happen to be passing Borneo again, d'ya think you could put us ashore? There must be some way of getting home that allows a man to get a bit of the old shut-eye."

The light from the blazing destroyer abruptly extinguished. Where she had been, a column of steam and smoke rose and drifted lazily toward them. The show was over. It was time to leave the theater before friends of the departed cast came along to give the front-row audience a going-over. *Harder* stood northward with all four diesels on the line. The battery needed charging, but *Harder* needed distance even more urgently.

Thirty minutes later, radar picked up an enemy patrol plane coming up from astern. *Harder* made one of her famed 30-second dives. No bombs dropped.

"That birdman certainly had us spotted," Dealey remarked to Frank Lynch. "He's undoubtedly reported us on a northerly course. So let's head south again just to confuse them."

Harder took a half-hour break in the concealing depths, then once more came to the surface headed back into the scene of trouble. This time Dealey put two engines to work charging. For thirty-five minutes it rammed amperes into the battery.

"Plane close aboard to starboard!"

Less than a mile away, a twin-float biplane, skimming along at no more than 100 feet of altitude, bore down on the submarine starkly visible in the brilliant moonlight.

"Left full rudder!" Dealey roared. "Clear the bridge! Dive! Dive!"

He found time to be thankful that the attacker was a slow traveler. The one-mile distance gave them nearly a minute to get under. They needed every second of it. At 150 feet, the first bomb fell reassuringly far off target. But the second blasted close enough to restart the leak in the antenna trunk.

"Take her to 200 feet," Dealey directed. Suddenly, as it usually happens after a period of prolonged excitement, the physical letdown came. Sam Dealey realized he was almost out on his feet, and knew that his crew must feel the same way.

"Secure all hands except the watch standers," he told Lynch. "This outfit needs a rest."

He had barely completed his instructions when sonar reported propeller noises coming their way with a turn count of 12 knots. For a moment, Dealey was tempted. But he instantly realized that a crew as weary as his might make a fatal error.

"Nothing doing," he decided. "Rig for silent running and let him go."

He turned to the officer of the deck.

"Call me an hour before sunrise."

Half falling down the ladder to the control room, he groped his way to his stateroom and fell asleep as he dropped into his bunk. For three hours he could sleep if the Japanese were willing to let him. They apparently were.

At twenty minutes to five Dealey was back in the conning tower. The midwatch had been relieved forty minutes earlier, and he was heartened to see that most of the strain had gone from the faces of the new watch standers as a result of their all too brief period of rest. He brought the ship up to radar and periscope depth. Nothing appeared in either. He knew that they faced another day of submerged running, for by now old Ozawa must be implementing with the direst threats his orders to get rid of the submarines that were whittling his destroyer fleet away. Dealey brought *Harder* to the surface, ordered two engines on charge and all air-induction valves opened. The atmosphere in the submarine had reached the lower limits of safety.

At best two-engine speed, *Harder* stood toward the entrance of Tawitawi Bay. Dealey was determined to get a look at the Mobile Fleet and report any evidence of movement. But unless a friendly storm showed up to shield them for surface running during daylight hours it would be nightfall before they could arrive off the fleet anchorage.

Morning twilight crept their way in a cloudless sky. To westward only endless blue prevailed in the area from which the monsoon wind would bring a storm if there was to be one. Resignedly he took *Harder* below to creep at economical speed toward their destination so near in distance but so far away in time. It would be a trying period, for the flat smoothness of the sea made it inadvisable to break the tedium too frequently with sights through the periscope. As the sun rose higher, *Harder* went deeper lest, deprived of the visual shield of waves, she be sighted by patrolling aircraft.

At nine in the morning, Dealey ordered her up to periscope depth for a quick look around, a move forced by the need for checking their position. The shore reference points were distressingly familiar, for *Harder* was making good only a little over one knot against the adverse current. Swinging the periscope toward the still distant entrance to Tawitawi, he sighted the upper works of two destroyers patrolling across the mouth of the bay, too far away for any hope of working *Harder* into attack position without surfacing in the brilliant sunshine. And that would have meant suicide. Reluctantly he took his ship below to continue her plodding advance toward the point only 10 miles away. It would take nearly eight hours. Eight hours of needed rest for his crew. Eight hours of irritating inaction for Sam Dealey.

Periodically throughout the day sonar picked up the screws of the patrolling destroyers coming nearer, but not near enough, and then receding as they marched and countermarched to shield the immobilized Mobile Fleet. Inside *Harder* no sonar gear was needed to pick up the echoing snores of weary men enjoying the first period of sustained inaction since they had first approached Sibutu Passage four days and four sunken Japanese destroyers ago. A destroyer a day. A record never before approached in the history of submarine warfare.

"Half hour to sunset, sir."

The voice came out of a deep, dark silence. Out of a misty void periodically lit up by the flash of exploding ships. Out of the tiny world of the conning tower in which Sam Dealey had fallen asleep, his head on the chart table.

"Thank you." He smiled a bit apologetically as though it had been wrong for his tired mind and body to have yielded to overpowering weariness.

160

From the far side of the conning tower, near the helmsman's station, Frank Lynch grinned at him.

"If you'd do a little more of that sort of thing, maybe the Japs would get a little sleep, too."

"Anything stirring?" Sam asked.

"Just our patrolling friends churning up the water," Lynch told him. "We're getting close in now. Estimate they were within 4 miles on their last reach our way."

Four miles would have been close enough for a submerged approach under good conditions. But conditions were not good with a battery nearing exhaustion after continuous cruising for a whole day. The spurt of speed needed to get into attack position would leave them little to make good their escape. But Dealey was already making plans for those destroyers' future as soon as darkness would permit *Harder* to open out on the surface.

"Heavy propeller noises of many ships!" It was the sonar operator reporting urgently over the intercom.

"How many do you make out?" Dealey demanded.

"They're too mixed to tell, sir," he answered. "Sounds like some big stuff, maybe even battleships. There are some destroyer noises, too."

"Sixty feet," Dealey spoke. "Up scope."

He walked the periscope rapidly through its complete arc.

"Down scope! Battle stations, torpedo!"

The sight that greeted his eyes in that hurried sweep was as awe-inspiring as it was threatening. The giant battleships *Yamato* and *Musashi*, four *Atago*-class cruisers, and nine destroyers were standing out from Tawitawi with eight float seaplanes circling overhead on antisubmarine patrol. From reports of earlier reconnaissance, Dealey knew that two *Kongo*-class battleships, three aircraft carriers, and a dozen more destroyers were still inside the anchorage.

To the task-force commanders of our own fleet moving in for the Marianas invasion, the sortie of the Mobile Fleet was vital information. Dealey could take *Harder* deep, come up after dark to track the enemy forces by radar, and get off the all-important contact report. But that program would involve leaving all those nice targets for somebody else to sink.

To attack meant to drain almost the last ampere from their tired battery in a high-speed approach and then be almost helpless to maneuver for escape. Unless . . .

"Up scope!"

The man at the periscope-elevating control tensed for the order to send it back down. In a calm sea only a few miles from an enemy force even a short exposure was risky business. But the order did not come. Dealey seemed to be inviting detection. He was.

"High-speed propeller noises approaching! Turn count 35 knots!" It was the sonar operator shouting over the intercom.

"Excellent." Dealey smiled. "His coming to us saves our battery. Bow tubes ready. Set for 6 feet. Now, down scope."

The disappearance of the scope would make the destroyer slow down in order to pick up his now hidden target on listening gear. A slower approach made Dealey's fire-control problem less complicated.

"Turn count down to 15 knots," sonar promptly reported.

"Up scope."

The destroyer was pointed right for *Harder*, about a mile away and a little on the starboard bow.

"Right standard rudder," Dealey ordered in the easy manner of an officer conning his ship up a well-marked and familiar channel. *Harder's* bow swung toward the oncoming destroyer.

"Steady as you go," Dealey told the helmsman.

"Range . . . mark!"

There was no need to record the bearing. It was dead ahead.

"Set," Sam Logan reported from the TDC.

"Let 'em go!"

"Six away," Logan told him.

"Emergency! Pull the plug!" Dealey's voice carried a note of real urgency. "Right full rudder!"

Harder did her best to imitate a stone. At 80 feet she was doing very well when she got an assist from above, a devastating blast that shattered the depth gauge, sprung the antenna trunk, and blew open the main air-induction valve to send sea water cascading into the forward engine room. She had been directly under the destroyer when the torpedo found its mark.

In momentary darkness when the main lighting circuit cut out, *Harder* plunged crazily downward. The emergency lighting came on somewhere about 100 feet below test depth. The disciplined hands of her crew brought her to an even keel.

In the silence of the conning tower, the voice of the sonar operator came over the intercom.

"High-speed propellers have stopped."

Their taut nerves relaxed in a roar of laughter that echoed and spread through the control room. Then came the reports from one compartment after another. *Harder* was hurt, but her wounds were healing rapidly under the ministrations of men who knew their ship as a surgeon knows the body on his operating table.

For the next two hours a raging enemy blew holes in the Celebes Sea with bombs, with depth charges, and even occasionally with shellfire aimed at imaginary periscopes that appeared before the eyes of desperate, frightened lookouts. At 300 feet, the men of *Harder* listened and occasionally chuckled. It was a terrific joke on the Japanese. The climactic payoff of a five-destroyer joke that had taken just five days to bring about. Even the veterans of the Borneo jungle joined in the fun. Oddly enough, they became more confident that these trouble-seeking lunatics would really get them home.

At midnight, June 10, 1944, *Harder* reported by radio the sortie of the Mobile Fleet from Tawitawi. Along the possible routes from Tawitawi to the Philippine Sea, other Pacific Fleet submarines raced into position to report Admiral Ozawa's movements and to whittle down the strength of his force.

For his history-making fight against an overwhelmingly powerful enemy, Comdr. Sam Dealey was awarded the Congressional Medal of Honor by President Roosevelt. But he and *Harder* had already departed Australia on their sixth war patrol before the medal got there.

They did not return.

While not a war story, the Nautilus *transit of the North Pole under the great Arctic ice pack is one of the most stirring events in submarine history. Here is* Nautilus' *"Moment of Truth" as written by her commanding officer.*

Piercing the Pole

WILLIAM R. ANDERSON, COMMANDER, U.S. NAVY, AND CLAY BLAIR, JR.

Two hours south of the Pole, a wave of unchecked excitement swept through *Nautilus.* Every man was up and about, and unabashedly proud to be aboard. Frank Adams, staring intently at the electronic gear, uttered a word often employed by *Nautilus* men who have exhausted all ordinary expressions to sum up their reaction to the never ending *Nautilus* triumphs: "Fan-damn-tastic."

When we crossed the Pole, of course, no bells would ring, nor would we feel a bump. Only our instruments could tell us how close we had come. Since we had made the decision to cross the Pole, we were determined to hit it precisely on the nose. Along with Navigator Shep Jenks and his assistant, Chief Petty Officer Lyle B. Rayl, I had stationed myself in the Attack Center, and although we were almost as far north as man can go on this planet, we were literally sweating over the charts and electronic position indicators, making minute, half-degree adjustments at the helm.

The hour by *Nautilus* clocks, which were still set on Seattle time, was 1900, or seven o'clock in the evening. Our nuclear engine, which up to then had pushed *Nautilus* more than 124,000 miles, was purring smoothly. Our electronic log, or speedometer needle, was hovering above 20 knots, the depth gauge needle about 400 feet. Our sensitive sonar indicated that the endless polar ice pack was running between 8 and 80 feet thick. Above the ice, we imagined, the polar wind was howling across its trackless, barren stamping ground, grinding massive floes one upon the other.

By then we had been under ice for sixty-two hours. Obviously, it was not possible to take the usual fix on heavenly bodies to determine our position, so we were navigating primarily by dead reckoning. This means that we were spacing our speed and course on the chart and plotting our position every half-hour or so, accordingly. Our bottom soundings, sometimes useful in submerged navigating, did not help, of course, in this uncharted, unsounded area. Our precision fathometer had indicated differences of as much as 8,000 feet at those rare points where soundings were made, so we could not rely on it. Our only check on our navigating was the inertial navigator. At the exact moment we crossed the Pole, we knew, the instrument would give a positive indication. Tom Curtis moved closer to his dials and scopes as we drew near.

A mile south of the Pole, I told Jenks to inform me when we were four-tenths of a mile from the Pole as indicated by the electronic log. The mileage indicator was moving rapidly. It was only a matter of seconds. *Nautilus* crewmen had gathered in the Attack Center and the Crew's Mess.

On Jenks' mark, I stepped up to the mike of the ship's public-address system:

"All hands—this is the captain speaking . . . In a few moments *Nautilus* will realize a goal long a dream of mankind—the attainment by ship of the North Geographic Pole. With continued Godspeed, in less than two days we will record an even more significant historic first: the completion of a rapid transpolar voyage from the Pacific to the Atlantic Ocean.

"The distance to the Pole is now precisely four-tenths of a mile. As we approach, let us pause in silence dedicated with our thanks for the blessings that have been ours during this remarkable voyage —our prayers for lasting world peace, and in solemn tribute to those who have preceded us, whether in victory or defeat."

The jukebox was shut off, and at that moment a hush literally fell over the ship. The only sound to be heard was the steady staccato of pinging from our sonars steadily watching the bottom, the ice, and the dark waters ahead.

I glanced again at the distance indicator and gave a brief countdown to the crew. "Stand by. 10 . . . 6 . . . 4 . . . 3 . . . 1. MARK! August 3, 1958. Time, 2315 (11:15 P.M. Eastern Daylight Saving Time). For the United States and the United States Navy, the North Pole." I could hear cheers in the Crew's Mess.

I looked anxiously at Tom Curtis. He was smiling. The inertial navigator had switched precisely as expected, positively confirming that we had crossed the exact North Pole. Curtis sang out: "As a matter of fact, Captain, you might say we came so close we pierced the Pole."

I stood for a moment in silence, awestruck at what *Nautilus* had achieved. She had blazed a new submerged northwest passage, vastly decreasing the sea-travel time for nuclear submarines from the Pacific to the Atlantic, one that could be used even if the Panama Canal were closed. When and if nuclear-powered cargo submarines are built, the new route would cut 4,900 miles and thirteen days off the route from Japan to Europe. *Nautilus* had opened a new era, completely conquered the vast, inhospitable Arctic. Our instruments were, for the first time, compiling an accurate and broad picture of the Arctic Basin and its approaches. *Nautilus'* achievement was dramatic proof of United States leadership in at least one important branch of science; and it would soon rank alongside or above the Russian sputnik in the minds of millions. Lastly, for the first time in history a ship had actually reached the North Pole. And never had so many men—116—been gathered at the Pole at one time.

I was proud of what *Nautilus* had done, yet I felt no sense of personal triumph or achievement. That we had reached the Pole was the work and support of many people. My reaction, frankly, was an overwhelming feeling of relief that after months and months of preparation and two unsuccessful probes we had finally made it.

Precisely at the Pole, for the record, I made note of some statistics which may or may not prove useful. The water temperature was 32.4 degrees Fahrenheit. The depth of the sea was 13,410 feet, exactly 1,927 feet deeper than reported by Ivan Papanin, a Russian who landed there, he claims, in an airplane in 1937. (In 1909 Admiral Peary had found the depth "greater than 9,000 feet.") At the exact Pole our ice detectors noted a pressure ridge extending 25 feet down.

After crossing the Pole, I made my way forward to join in the "North Pole Party" in the Crew's Mess. My first act was to pay modest tribute to the man who, more than any other, had made our historic voyage possible: the President of the United States. A few minutes before, I had written him a message. It concluded: "I hope, sir, that you will accept this letter as a memento of a voyage of importance to the United States." In the Mess, before seventy crew members of *Nautilus*, I signed this letter, and one to Mrs. Eisenhower, who had christened the ship.

Other events followed. A "North Pole" cake prepared especially by leading Commissaryman Jack L. Baird, was cut, distributed, and wolfed down. Electrician's Mate First Class James Sordelet raised his right hand and became the first man in history to reenlist at the North Pole. In a special North Pole ceremony eleven other men, having passed the rigid written and oral examinations, were "qualified in nuclear submarines." The prize-winning title to correspond to Shellbacks and Bluenoses was announced: Panopo, short for "Pacific to the Atlantic via the North Pole." A "North Pole" postcard, stamped with the special North Pole cachet, was distributed to all hands. On the reverse side was a cartoon by McNally showing a sailor in a bathing suit standing on a small block of ice leaning against a striped "North Pole." The card read: "Greetings from Sunny Panama." All during these proceedings, movie and still cameras whirred and clicked.

Then a distinguished citizen "came aboard." It was our talented McNally, dressed as Santa Claus. What a sight he made! Red vegetable coloring was splattered on his face. His whiskers were made of medical cotton, and a pillow was stuffed inside his Santa Claus suit, made of flag bunting.

Santa berated us for entering his private domain during the vacation season. He chided us particularly for our failure to abide by his restriction on the use of garbage disposal units by submerged transiting submarines! I pleaded ignorance and promised on behalf of all the ship's company children to abide by all his rules henceforth.

That done, Santa Claus relaxed and became his usual jovial self. He listened very patiently as one of the fathers in the crew, Chief Engineman Hercules H. Nicholas, argued that the behavior of our children was absolutely beyond reproach. Santa promised, in light of our personal visit to the North Pole, that the coming Christmas season would be merry and lucrative for all our children.

Perspiring heavily, Santa finally said, "Well, I've got to go back to the Pole to make sure the elves are working." And with that our extraordinary party ended. The jukebox was turned back as men drifted to their bunks for a little rest.

An "extra" edition of the ship's newspaper was published that day, entitled "*Nautilus Express*—North Pole Edition." It was unusually mild in tone and contained nothing libelous, which is an indication, I believe, that all hands were deeply moved by *Nautilus'* triumph.

In two world wars, German submarines almost forced the surrender of Britain and her allies before the United States entered the war. U.S. submarines in the Pacific strangled the lifelines of the widespread Japanese Empire. Today, at the beginning of the second half of the twentieth century, submarine commanders hold the potential destruction of the world in their hands. This bone-chilling account of the United States Polaris submarines shows why.

Apocalypse Below

EDITORS OF NAVY TIMES

ON A warm, cloudy Tuesday, November 15, 1960, the giant submarine *George Washington* pushed down the Cooper River to leave astern the wharves, the balconied mansions, and the church spires of Charleston, South Carolina. Ahead lay the seeming infinity of the Atlantic Ocean.

On the conning tower of this 380-foot-long, 5,900-ton monster stood her combat-hardened, eminently capable captain, Comdr. James B. Osborn, forty-two-year-old Missourian. He puffed on a cigar, waiting to attain a designated area 65 miles at sea where he would "take her down." When he did so he would be writing a new and especially sober chapter in the history of submarining.

Embarking on no ordinary voyage, Osborn was at the "con" of the first SSBN (submarine ballistic missile nuclear) to go on patrol. Each of her 16 Polaris missiles was easily capable of destroying an entire city, harbor, or military installation—from a compact supply depot or missile launching site to a sprawling infantry camp or even airfield. Osborn and his crew of more than 100 could fire these deadly "birds" while submerged far below the surface and at targets 1,200 miles distant.

In other words, he could heave-to well off the west coast of Europe, even above the Arctic Circle, and obliterate, for example, Leningrad.

169

"The *George Washington* and her following sister ships," declared President Eisenhower, "possess a power and relative invulnerability which will make suicidal any attempt by an aggressor to attack the free world by surprise."

Navy Secretary Thomas S. Gates added that the submarine "opens a new era in naval warfare and greatly enhances the overall capabilities of our armed forces."

The "new era" almost commenced in 1942, at Peenemünde on the Baltic, when a small rocket was successfully fired from a submerged German U-boat. Ernst Steinhoff, the young admiralty engineer who had conceived of the unique weapon, fortunately was frustrated in further research. The Nazis wished all of their efforts placed on the development of the V-2 rocket.

It was nearly fourteen years later, with the international temperature boiling once more, before the United States Navy exhumed Steinhoff's brilliant invention, rudimentary as it had been, and started winding up a true crash program to make underwater guided-missilery a reality. Its spark plug became a stocky, Texas-born redhead, William F. Raborn, Jr., former carrier pilot who had been an assistant to Rear Admiral John Sides when the latter was director of Navy research on guided missiles. Vice Admiral Raborn, former director of the Navy's Special Projects Office and presently Deputy Chief of Naval Operations, brought his project to fruition in the incredible period of four years. Three years ahead of schedule, he had produced operational missiles and the first of a fleet of submarines to launch them, supplanting the earlier Regulus, or V-1-like winged missile to be deck launched.

The hundred-million-dollar-plus Polaris submarines, for all their bulk, excellence of design, and great speed, which may unofficially be in the neighborhood of 50 knots, are nonetheless but the workhorses which lug the missiles to blast-off areas. The Polaris, described as "an instrument of national policy," is the ballerina of this operation.

A Navy spokesman noted:

"With almost unlimited submerged cruising range, and perseverance to the limit of crew endurance, the FBM (fleet ballistic missile) nuclear submarine is capable of extended submerged operation in the international waters of the world,

170

which comprise about 70 per cent of the earth's surface. Free of the need to surface or extend a snorkel above the surface for continuous operation, FBM nuclear submarines will remain hidden by an oceanic curtain, their locations unknown to any potential enemy. Their Polaris missiles, powered by solid propellant, will be ready for launch within minutes of receiving the command and without the need for long countdown. Mobile, hidden, ready for prompt but well-considered reaction, the FBM system will provide the United States with a virtually invulnerable and powerful war-deterrent force capable of striking almost any potential enemy target in the world with nuclear warheads.

"Polaris, named for the North Star, is a two-stage ballistic missile about 28 feet long, 4½ feet in diameter, and weighing about 30,000 pounds. It is powered by solid fuel rocket motors and guided by a self-contained inertial guidance system independent of any external commands or enemy interference. Each motor exerts thrust through four nozzles in the motor base. Thrust vector (direction control) is exercised by devices called jetevators. The solid-fueled Polaris is relatively simple to manufacture and requires little upkeep and maintenance in storage. The little attention required can be provided readily.

"Initially, the range of the missile is 1,200 nautical miles (1,380 statute miles). Future development will give the missile a range of more than 1,500 nautical miles by 1963. A further range increase to 2,500 miles is programmed. Meanwhile, the 1,200-mile missile and the unlimited cruising range of the nuclear submarine combine to give the FBM system an effective range within reach of almost all significant potential enemy targets in the world."

Each launching tube possesses its own air supply, independent of the other fifteen tubes. Their area within the submarine, once known as a magazine, is now dubbed, more colorfully, "Sherwood Forest." Whether the crews think of themselves as Robin Hoods is quite another consideration.

In this "forest" the "birds" are so arranged that their mechanisms can be inspected, and repairs and adjustments readily made at any time, at sea, or in port.

Polaris obviously has rewritten the books on naval warfare. In fact, it has crossed boundaries that a Mahan would have thought impregnable—all the way into the hitherto sacrosanct provinces of the Air Force, and of the Army's artillery and even infantry. Knowing the range, a field commander can conceivably call for supporting Polaris fire against any ground target from a submarine hove-to 1,000 miles offshore.

Such radical concepts obviously demand both an integrated and thoughtful strategy—and the No. 1 strategist for Polaris is Rear Admiral Ignatius J. Galantin, a soft-spoken, silver-haired Annapolis graduate, Class of '33, who grew up in Des Plaines, Illinois.

Deliberate and calculating, Galantin proved his fighting and planning abilities in his World War II submarine service. As commander of the USS *Halibut*, in the Pacific, he won the Navy Cross. "A skilled and aggressive leader," was but one of plaudits ringing from his citation. "Bold" and "determination" were among successive words of official tribute accompanying decorations as he destroyed or crippled many thousands of tons of enemy warships and transports.

The fact that he has spent almost his entire naval career with submarines has, perhaps surprisingly, not given Galantin a lopsided viewpoint at all.

"The development of our surface Navy must continue," he says. "Sea power is the keystone of our collective security system, of our defensive alliances, and it takes all forms of naval power to assure the control of the seas. The submarine is but a subordinate component of our overall naval warfare system. Some things the submarine can do better than any other vehicle, but it has limited means of gathering information and of influencing events on the surface or on land. After all, we are really seeking to control, not necessarily to destroy. Here, in the efficiency of its deterrent role, is where the Polaris submarine is most useful."

Galantin believes that the missile-firing submarine is a weapons system uniquely suited for American purposes. Because of its relative invulnerability, it permits deliberate and measured response, and is actually a stabilizing factor in the current politico-military situation. It is ideally suited to our national deterrent-retaliatory policy. Not doubting that Russia could ultimately duplicate our Polaris fleet should she so desire, Galantin nonetheless does not think such craft fit into her armament locker, committed to long-range, land-based rockets as she apparently is.

For that matter, he does not wholeheartedly accept the premise that the U.S.S.R. is aggressively minded. On the other hand, he considers that she may be manifesting her historic suspicion and distrust of other countries, obsessed with the notion that she is subject to surprise attack—in other words, a kind of national paranoid.

There are many others who are less confident than Galantin as to the Polaris and our other weapons as deterrents to actual armed conflict. Dr. Oskar Morgenstern, for example, professor of political philosophy at Princeton University and a consultant on defense to various organizations, is admittedly pessimistic. While expressing faith in Polaris, especially if its range can be trebled and if it can be launched from surface craft as well as submarines, he has asserted:

"The probability that a large-scale, devastating thermonuclear exchange will occur is greater than that it will not occur. No war has ever been averted by recourse to moral and religious constraints. On the contrary, many of the most cruel and bloody wars were fought over such issues. There is no hope that now, suddenly, new moral values can be evolved and become effective enough to take us away from the highly probable disaster. The only way now visible to stop war is a deterrence which will mean destruction for the aggressor."

The tacticians and theoreticians as well will continue to speculate on what might or could happen, but meanwhile the patrols must go on, carried out (as this is written) by five submarines operating out of Holy Loch, Scotland. They are the vanguard of forty or more, now either under trials, under construction, or on the drawing boards. They will be led in size by the giant, new-class *Lafayette*, which will displace 7,000 tons—the greatest underwater craft ever built. This great ship, whose keel was laid in January, 1961, in New London, Connecticut, by French Ambassador Herve Alphand, will also be an exception to the custom of naming Polaris submarines after famous Americans—though some hold Lafayette to be an adopted son since at least one of the original thirteen states conferred citizenship upon him.

The patrols from Holy Loch, the pretty cove at the foot of the Scottish highlands where the submarine tender *Proteus* anchors, are seemingly endless periods of underwater captivity, measured by nonsubmariner standards—sixty days without respite, lurking danger a constant shipmate. Submarines, as in the past, can fall victims to a variety of accidents as readily as they can to an enemy. However, submariners of all nations are used to living and working in their ships for long periods at sea, hence their insistence on quality in material, in workmanship, in personnel.

This strange, sardine-like existence, however, is made bearable for the sailors not only by the relative comfort and amplitude of accommodations but by the prospect of shore leave and reunions with their families for periods equal to their patrols. Each submarine is manned by two complete crews of 110–130 men each, designated "Blue" and "Gold." As the Blue crew of the *Ethan Allen* comes ashore, the Gold, seabags over shoulders, goes aboard. The submarine itself needs little turnaround time other than that necessary for minor adjustments and reprovisioning. Thus, relatively few men can keep these important, complex, and expensive ships on station, engaged the greatest part of the time in their vital, deadly serious mission.

Most of the submariners live in New London, and there Blue and Gold crewmen alternately rest, study, or take trips with their families for the sixty days or so they are at home. The very fact the sailors can plan ahead for their off-duty days makes for high morale, stability in domestic life, and a firm desire to stay with their demanding, lonesome, but rewarding branch of the service.

Indeed, these men look with compassion upon their shipmates of the surface fleet who wave good-bye for long months whenever the fleet weighs anchor.

The habits, the numerical size, and certainly the underwater domain of submarine crews have altered in giant leaps from *Turtle* to *Hunley* to *Holland* to the "S" boats of World War I to the *Gato* class of World War II to *Guppy* to *Nautilus* and finally to the mighty *Lafayette*.

Nonetheless, as strikingly profound as these changes have been, the concept of mission is the most radical of all the evolutions which have taken place in submarine design and employment.

City killer?

Bombarder of military bases?

Underwater snooper of enemy secrets?

Instrument of national policy?

A deterrent in itself?

As late as World War II these considerations would have been stamped visionary, and possibly quite impractical.

"War," wrote the strategist von Clausewitz a century and a half ago, "is an act of violence pushed to its utmost bounds."

The Polaris philosophy falls within this definition.

"The errors," postscripted the same Prussian general, "which proceed from a spirit of benevolence are the worst."

Indeed, the Polaris fleet can neither give nor accept quarter. It cannot, by its nature, inflict "just a little" damage upon the enemy, hoping it will hurt here and spare there. Once the "birds" scream upward from their "Sherwood Forest," the submarine, along with the nation, is committed.

The submarine, in spite of desultory efforts in opposite directions, is today an instrument of war, a vehicle from which the deep can now launch sudden havoc. In many respects, Polaris seemingly represents the fruition, the ultimate in naval power.

Apocalypse it surely is.

Whether the vision it provides is one of dawn or of everlasting darkness, certainly not even those who fathered the Polaris can be expected to say.

Index

178